T0113403

Praise for *Seven Steps to Heaven*

"Joyce Keller's new book is a must-read for all afterlife believers. She is a great professional who has contributed to the field of metaphysics."
—Jeffrey A. Wands, professional psychic and author of *The Psychic in You*

"*Seven Steps to Heaven* clearly describes, with tremendous insight, how easy and comforting it is to communicate with our loved ones and pets who are on the 'other side.' Of all the books on this subject, including my own, I put it up there toward the top of the list. A must-read!"
—Linda Georgian, author of *Communicating With the Dead*

"*Seven Steps to Heaven* describes seven straightforward ways you can communicate with loved ones who have passed on. With warmth, wit, and wisdom, Joyce Keller demonstrates how rewarding it can be to initiate a dialogue with spirits of deceased people and animals. If you've ever felt a need to talk to someone who's died, this book will inspire you to stay in touch!"
—Cynthia Sue Larson, author of *Aura Advantage*

"Joyce Keller proves to be a real angel with her *Seven Steps to Heaven*. If you've ever lost a loved one, this book is for you. Joyce is a winning writer with another winning book."
—Soupy Sales

"*Seven Steps to Heaven* speaks in practical terms of how each of us can benefit from the invisible support that surrounds all of us. Readers will appreciate its 'how-to' approach and benefit from its healing touch."
—George E. Dalzell, L.C.S.W., author of *Messages: Evidence for Life After Death*

Seven Steps to Heaven

How to Communicate with
Your Departed Loved Ones
in Seven Easy Steps

Joyce Keller

A FIRESIDE BOOK
Published by Simon & Schuster
New York London Toronto Sydney Singapore

FIRESIDE
Rockefeller Center
1230 Avenue of the Americas
New York, NY 10020

Fireside and colophon are registered trademarks
of Simon & Schuster, Inc.

For information regarding special discounts for bulk purchases,
please contact Simon & Schuster Special Sales at 1-800-456-6798
or business@simonandschuster.com.

Designed by Christine Weathersbee

Manufactured in the United States of America

10   9   8   7   6   5   4   3   2   1

Library of Congress Cataloging-in-Publication Data

Keller, Joyce (Joyce E.)
    Seven steps to heaven : how to commmunicate with your departed loved
ones in seven easy steps / Joyce Keller.
        p.   cm.
    "A Fireside book."
    Includes bibliographical references.
    1. Spiritualism. I. Title.
BF1261.2.K45 2003
133.9—dc21   2003053893

ISBN: 978-0-7432-2560-1

To God, our Creator

Acknowledgments

With appreciation for love and support from my editor, Marcela Landres, and Liz Bevilacqua; my agent and friend, June Rifkin Clark; Dr. Scott Keller; Joan Riggi; Joan Marie Powers; Joey Alcarese; Kris Soumas; Linnea Leaver; Martin Schwartz; John J. and Benita Silvestri; Florence Fayden; Tina Davis; Michelle Radz; Tina Mosetis; Betty Gross; Allyson Edelhertz; all of my loving, helpful, and dear relatives; Leah and Ilene Roth; our magnificent program director, Tom Ross; Soupy and Trudy Sales; Regis Philbin; and Oprah Winfrey.

A special acknowledgment to **Elaine Beardsley,** who edited this book.

Contents

Part Three

Loud and Clear: Beyond the Seven Steps

Opening

I am well aware that many will say that no one can possibly speak
with spirits and angels so long as he is living in a physical body.
Many say it is all fancy, others, that I recount such things to
win credence, while others will make other kinds of objection.
But I am undeterred by none of these, for I have seen,
I have heard, I have felt.

—Emanuel Swedenborg

My mother was a medium. Out of respect for our
departed loved ones, my parents and I spent a great deal of my childhood in cemeteries. What's really scary is that this seemed like a normal part of life to me. My parents believed that it was necessary to
visit the graves of their parents, grandparents, siblings, friends, and
God-knows-who-else, at least once a week. I spent a lot of my childhood in the backseat of my parents' car as they drove slowly through
various Brooklyn, Queens, and New York cemeteries, stopping from
time to time to place flowers on loved ones' graves.

The confusion that these trips caused me reached an apex when I
was about four years old. My parents had failed or simply forgotten

to tell me the real purpose of a cemetery. As we drove slowly around Calvary Cemetery on this day, my mom pointed to a mausoleum and asked my dad, "Joe, what do you think about buying one of those?"

As my dad stopped the car in front of this tiny, dark, bleak, gray stone house with no windows, I thought, "They must be joking . . . how can the four of us live in *that?* There's no room for my bike or anything . . . wait a minute . . . there are no kids around here for me to play with . . . no dogs . . . no Good Humor trucks . . ." I started to cry.

My mom looked at me in the backseat, and asked, "What's wrong?"

"I don't want to live here!" I cried.

My parents looked at each other and laughed. My mom said, "Oh, Joy, honey, only dead people's bodies are here!"

"Huh?" I said. "What do you mean?"

My father rolled his eyes and began driving while my mom put me on her lap in the front seat. This was a red-letter moment, as she then introduced me to the world of the seen and the unseen. She had my complete attention, because she presented death from the viewpoint of a medium. She explained that life and energy can never be destroyed because we never really die. "People are not under the ground, just their tired worn-out bodies. Their spirit goes with God to a very beautiful place that's filled with angels and heavenly light. We leave the physical body behind, usually because it's very old and tired," she explained.

She continued, "Trust me, Joy, the other side is very peaceful and pleasant. No sadness, sickness, or suffering." She wiped away a couple of remaining tears and hugged me, adding, "So stop worrying. We're not moving to the cemetery. Now, let's go have some ice cream!"

At other times I would sit on my mother's bed as she talked about dreams and seeing spirits. It was such a part of my life: Mother speaking about departed loved ones, how not to be afraid, how there was no barrier between us. She communicated with spirits as if they were actually in the room: "See? Aunt Mary's over there, and there's Grandpa, walking by and smiling." To me, it seemed normal as she wished them well and blessed them.

Spirit contact was a part of my life—no beginning and end—just always there. The worlds blended together, the seen and the unseen. I had insightful parents. They were full of surprises and amazing answers. They could always keep things in the right perspective. They were true life teachers while they were here, and as you will see, continued as spirit teachers in the beyond. Because of my parents, by the age of four, my lifelong odyssey of traveling through seen and unseen worlds had begun.

As I grew older, I wanted more information on spirit communication. As a teenager, I visited mediums and ventured further into this realm. I entered a world that was filled with wonder, mystery, and unfortunately, fraud. I soon realized that discernment was the key to enjoying a truthful world of spirit contact. In other words, you can't believe everything you see and hear, even if it comes from the most "respected" of mediums.

In my continued search, I scoured books and directories, and eventually discovered spiritualist centers, with classes, workshops, and sessions that concentrate on spirit communication. One of the oldest in the country is Camp Chesterfield, in Indiana. Another is Lily Dale, near Niagara Falls, New York. Silver Belle, in Ephrata, Pennsylvania, which is unfortunately no longer in existence, was my favorite. My husband, Jack, and I went there many times. There, we found a controlled professional atmosphere for spirit communication. Were our experiences at these centers always aboveboard and honest? Probably not completely, but it was fascinating, and a great test of discernment.

The mediums at Silver Belle were especially developed in the art of spirit connection and conducted séances in safe, blessed, dark rooms. They were professional. There was no intrusion of unwanted light or sound, and the medium's ectoplasm (see the Glossary at the end of the book) was effectively used as a conduit for spirit expression. It was safe in that it was done by experienced mediums who knew how to control the energy and present the entities so that people would not be frightened. It was fun, entertaining, and it appeared to be authentic. I say *appeared*, because I could tell when it was not true spirit communication, when the energy being expressed did not feel quite right, was inaccurate, or was off the mark.

Another way I could tell that the messages were authentic was when my maiden name was used. My name was Tagliarini, and could not easily have been made up or guessed. Believe me, my name was spelled out by spirits quite a number of times, and besides making me chuckle, it always made me feel that the contact was authentic. There were no messages for phony "Bobs," nor any lines like, "Is there an *M* in the room? I have a message for an *M*. Or wait, maybe it's a message *from* an *M*. Does anyone know an *M?*" To me there is nothing more frustrating or deceptive than a so-called medium who goes through the alphabet.

At spiritualist centers there was a wide variety of exciting spirit expression. There were spirit messages from loved ones, apologies, greetings of love, expressions of lost opportunities, and an eagerness to reconnect with those who were left on earth. There were gifts from spirits, known as *apports,* and most impressively, materializations.

My first experience with full-fledged materialization occurred shortly after I read the amazing book *Autobiography of a Yogi,* by Indian yogi Paramahansa Yogananda. I found this book thrilling and spoke of it often to Jack and close friends. While I was attending a contact session at Silver Belle a short time after I read this book, Yogananda, who died in 1952, appeared and called my name out of a circle of twenty people. I was stunned. His white translucent figure floated directly toward me. My heart beat so loudly I could hear it in my ears as Yogananda stopped in front of me and said clearly, "Joyce, thank you for your appreciation of my book and for speaking so kindly of it to so many people." It is noteworthy that no one at Silver Belle knew me or of my enthusiasm for Yogananda and his teachings at that time.

This was just one of many incredible experiences that I had at the spiritualist centers. I was also privileged to have been a part of photo séances, known as "silk circles."* Some of the incredible

---

*"Silk circles" are so called because photos from the spirit world are manifest on pieces of silk material. It "precipitates" onto the material and is a mysterious gift from the world of spirit.

photos I received from the world of spirit are included in this book. One of my favorites is the photo of one of my teachers, Mataji. Mataji is the sister of Babaji, who in India is known as the Holy Father. She is the Hindu counterpart of the Christian Blessed Mother. Mataji looks the same way in her spirit photo as I have seen her in my dreams and meditations. I was surprised to receive the photo, until I remembered that in my meditation, Mataji had promised me that I would have a photo of her. Incredibly, she kept her word.

I tell you this because, while you carry on your own spiritual search, you must not view anyone else's opinion as an endorsement or a condemnation. Use your own best sense. Be skeptical. Always test the spirits by asking about things that no one else knows. But be open also to the good things that can and will happen.

I have had the blessing of being taught by a number of masterful teachers, living and not, whose wisdom is shared in this book. One of these is Babaji, the Indian Holy Father, who has come to me often with help and inspiration. Paramahansa Yogananda, who is considered to have been one of the greatest spiritual leaders to have ever been on this planet, is also part of my band of spiritual teachers. He is credited for bringing the teachings of India and "Kriya Yoga," or the yoga of enlightenment, to the United States in a way that was easily understood and illuminating. Yogananda has come to me many times, not only manifesting in a physical form, but also in my dreams, meditations, and as inspiration for much of my spiritual writing.

I found another great instructor in Edgar Cayce. Cayce was known as "the sleeping prophet," because he would connect with the spirit world in a trance. In the sleep state he could be given the name of anyone in the world and be able to tell in great detail what his physical, mental, emotional, or spiritual problems were, what karmic or past life experience was causing his problem, and how the problem could be remedied. Cayce, who lived in the early part of the twentieth century, was an authority on spiritual contact, and his life's work inspired a legacy of teachings in this area as well as on karma, reincarnation, and spiritual, mental, and physical health.

My spiritual quest, which began when I was four, eventually evolved into a lifelong endeavor. For the past sixteen years I have been hosting *The Joyce Keller Show** in the New York area with my husband, Jack, and it has become America's longest-running, live, psychic-advice call-in show. Our show specializes in connecting listeners to their departed loved ones and offers intuitive advice, support, and healing for all manner of problems. We've had a wide spectrum of guests on this show, ranging from Regis Philbin to Soupy Sales to world-renowned psychics, mediums, and healers. What I've learned from the show is something that I always suspected: nothing is as powerful as addressing the problems or situation facing the caller. Listeners are able to relate to the problems of others, because we learn from each other's issues and mistakes.

There have been amazing reports from my listeners and television viewers, many of whose spirit contact experiences are recounted in the following pages. Those who have made contact describe exceptional feelings of relaxation and peace when contact occurs with departed loved ones.

Like you, these listeners and viewers seek to bridge the gap, to reach from the physical to the higher, nonphysical world. The new age of awareness and enlightenment tells us that with God, all things are possible. Once we know how it can be done, we can practice spirit connection ourselves. It is indeed safe, healing, and very therapeutic.

In India, religious ascetics spend extensive time practicing stringent discipline and control in order to "pierce the bindu," or to part the veil between the physical and nonphysical worlds. The

**The Joyce Keller Show* is on WGBB 1240 AM Radio. It is also on the World Wide Web at *www.wgbb.com.*

New Zealand Maori tribe pierces the bindu by undergoing physical pain, bodily deprivation and extremes in temperature, and by using hallucinogenic drugs. Hindus and other religious groups achieve connection with the higher planes by employing equally severe techniques. Many religions honor suffering saints and martyrs who have gone to extremes to bring about clear spirit contact. We will not recommend any of these methods in this book! Instead, you will find methods that are tested, therapeutic, straightforward, and safe. These methods are embodied in my Connection Technique, an approach that I have developed over many years of practice.

Though at many times in my life I went to great distances and trouble to make spirit contact, I eventually realized that contact was being made all around me, at all times. My spiritual quest now brings me here to you, to broaden awareness through this book. By tuning in, you will begin noticing messages from beyond. It's a matter of building openness, sensitivity, and doing what it takes to become more aware of the conscious and unconscious world around you. With practice, you will experience spirit communication yourself and not have to rely on other parties.

Remember, life and energy can never be destroyed because we never really die. People are not under the ground—just their bodies. Their spirit goes to a place that's filled with light. When we leave the physical body behind, it is merely to continue the journey in another dimension.

Remember, too, to test the spirits. Always ask if they are "of God," or of the "highest good in the universe," or of a high, positive vibration. Successful spirit contact is usually accompanied by cosmic consciousness and higher awareness. There is no barrier between the seen and unseen worlds.

Not long after my mother died, she came to me, as she had done a few times at this point, in a dream. She was perspiring and seemed to be quite warm. After standing in front of me for a few moments, she laughed and said, "Oh, you think I'm down there (pointing downward) because I'm so hot! No. I'm going through a purification process. It will help to cleanse me of the earth's vibrations, so I can make a faster, easier transition. The heat is a good thing!"

I asked, "Ma, where are you?"

She said, "I'm in the temporal zone. It's an area that's right outside the earth plane, and beyond the astral. Have to go now. Love you."

Then she was gone, and I didn't see her again for a few months in earth's time. When she appeared again, it was to offer more information, love, and assurance.

That is what I am here to offer you. My journey in the spirit realm has been an extraordinary one and is far from over; yours may be just beginning. Embark on your journey knowing that you have the support of many teachers who offer you light and love as you seek contact with your loved ones.

Om shanti, peace and love be with you always,

Joyce

Don't Be Afraid

Don't be afraid
God will take your hand;
Follow the light
To his heavenly land.

Don't be afraid
God guides from birth;
We're in his kingdom
Whether it's heaven or earth.

Don't be afraid
To reconnect with those lost
The love continues
Even after we've crossed.

—JOYCE KELLER

PART I

Opening the Lines of Communication

The bitterest tears shed over graves are
for words left unsaid, and deeds left undone.

—Harriet Beecher Stowe

ONE

Clearing Away
Misconceptions

Because I could not stop for death,

he kindly stopped for me.

The carriage held but just ourselves,

and immortality.

—EMILY DICKINSON

Who among us hasn't lost a loved one? What would we give for just one more conversation, one more joke, one more shared secret? One more chance to apologize or explain what was really in our heart and mind? Well, I understand. In my many years of taking calls on radio and TV, the most frequent request is always for spirit contact and communication.

Every other week it seems at least one book on spirit validity has appeared on the *New York Times* bestseller list. Nearly all of us are yearning for someone we've loved and lost who has passed away. In this book, I will lead you through my Connection Technique, which encompasses seven steps to safely make spirit communication possible and enjoyable. This system is the result of years of refining techniques that work well for people practicing spirit communication. I have combined these with my own methods, which I will share with you here.

Most people in our society believe that some magical and totally mysterious transformation occurs when we pass over. Spirit contact is much easier if it is not so glorified and mystified. It's a natural part of life!

What Seven Steps to Heaven *Is Not:*
A textbook
A collection of case studies
A history of spiritualism in America
A high-concept, impossible-to-understand workbook
Self-aggrandizing
Stiff and misleading
Depressing

What Seven Steps to Heaven *Is:*
A lighthearted approach to a difficult subject
Enlightening (we hope!)
Accurate
A practical guide on how to contact those
   you've loved and lost

Seven Steps to Heaven is a concise, fun, easy-to-follow (did we say uplifting?) guide on how to contact those you've loved and lost.

I have been developing this Connection Technique over the last thirty years. I have used it successfully on my own radio and TV shows, as well as on *The Oprah Winfrey Show, Live with Regis, Sally Jessy Raphael, Geraldo, Entertainment Tonight,* FOX TV, and other shows. It is, I believe, the first time you will see anything like this in print or in practice.

Here's the breaking news: You don't need to enlist the services of an expensive, and possibly fraudulent, go-between to connect with your departed loved ones. For those who prefer not to spend endless hours, not to mention unlimited money, hunting for psychics, gurus, and the like, I give you dependable and tested techniques for putting the art of spirit communication into practice. You can use these tools to equip yourself for contact with the departed. Best of all, you can make the desired contact yourself, safely and easily.

I hope that this book will give you the tools to get started and lead you to discover how after-death communication can benefit you.

Most of all, I hope you will be inspired by *Seven Steps to Heaven*.

Let's Begin with a Smile, Okay?

I know that many of you who read this book are dealing with tremendous feelings of sadness and loss. I truly sympathize with you. I sincerely hope that this book will help alleviate your pain. I pray that you will be in less emotional distress. But before you finish this book, I want you to laugh, because laughter is one of the most powerful life forces and it connects us to the highest energy in the universe.

Why Does Spirit Communication Seem Difficult?

Spirit communication seems difficult because most people don't know the rules. Native Americans and many other groups of people find spirit communication as natural, safe, and easy as breathing. For them, there is nothing to debate, since it is a natural part of life.

In our society, spirit communication is shrouded in fear, so no one tells us how to go about doing it. What we don't understand, see, or touch with a feeling of familiarity and comfort, we are inclined to fear. Frightening movies and ghost stories have fueled feelings of fearing the unknown and unseen. However, what we understand and bring out into the light of day we no longer fear. In this book, you will learn how to safely align your energies so that your vibrations are compatible with the spirit world. Connection will feel natural.

Another reason spirit connection seems difficult is that people in our society are taught from an early age that spirit communication is ridiculous, impossible, or that it is dangerous and not to be encouraged. At a very early age, we learn to ignore spirit messages, dreams, and impulses. Individuals are considered to be unintelligent, gullible, or worse yet, insane, if they claim to communicate with those who have passed on. Yet in other countries—such as Brazil, Russia, and China—people encourage and work with intuitively talented children and adults.

There is no question that some societies view psychic individuals as having a below-average IQ. Why can't people be intuitive *and* intelligent? Given the choice between being considered crazy or considered not too bright, people don't talk about or encourage intuitive talents. No wonder we stifle the desire to connect.

As if all of this is not enough to turn off mediumistic talents, certain religious schools punish children who have psychic abilities. Some Western religions even pound home the message that spirit contact is "demonic." Yet nothing is more healing or divinely transcendent to the spirit of humans who have lost loved ones than the experience of reconnection. This thinking is not within the capability of some Western religions. Some claim that it is against the laws of God to believe in or to participate in after-death communication. Some religions perceive psychic mediums who connect grieving people with their departed loved ones as threats. But, really, what stops organized religion from doing the same thing?

Truly, mass media has not always contributed to our feelings of comfort and security about spirit interaction either. On the bright side, movies like *Ghost* and *The Sixth Sense* have helped turn the tide and have shown that spirit contact can be therapeutic and safe. Most of the frightening movies, articles, speakers, and books that tout the negative side of spirit communication are not truly authentic and are made for sensational shock appeal, or as a means of increasing the naysayers' power. Fortunately, things are changing for the better in this society. Our level of consciousness and awareness is increasing.

Finally, some of us think that only psychically "gifted" people connect with the spirit world. It may seem crazy or impossible for ordinary people to experience connection. I assure you, it isn't. The truth is that half of what is required to contact departed loved ones is simply the desire to do so. The remaining half consists of gaining expertise through methods like those offered in this book.

Don't Cast Pearls Before Swine!

You may not want to share your desire for spirit communication with people who ridicule you or who attempt to limit you with their own limitations. Don't be victimized by the fears of others. If people snicker or put you down, keep your desire for spirit communication to yourself.

Still Not Sure?

Each night before going to sleep, open up your heart, mind, and spirit to God, the universe, your spirit teachers, your spirit loved ones . . . whatever is comfortable to you. Ask for proof. Ask for signs. There's nothing wrong with that.

Each day, pay attention to the little things that you might have previously missed. Look for signs that indicate that you are in successful communication with the spirit world. Look for small things that might contain messages. Throughout the day, whenever you think about it, take a deep breath, send out vibrations, and ask for spirit guidance, signs, or something that will prove to you that there is life after death. No matter what other people say, nothing is stronger proof than when you experience it yourself—and you will!

Now let's clear up some other misconceptions.

Death is perceived to be the end of an earthly existence,
but actually death is only a change in matter and form.
—AUTHOR UNKNOWN

What Is the Difference Between Psychics and Mediums?

A psychic is one who has extrasensory perception (ESP) that enables him or her to feel, sense, smell, see, or hear that which is not apparent to the five physical senses. This information may relate to the past, present, or future of you or persons close to you. Perceiving information about the future is called precognition. Some psychics can "read" impressions left on things (psychometry) or in places, such as crime scenes or in haunted areas. Some psychics or "sensitives," as they are also called, use dowsing rods to find things, like underground water or mineral deposits. A genuine and developed psychic is able to tap into your past, present, or future with a high degree of accuracy, but will not necessarily put you in contact with your departed loved ones.

On the other hand, a medium is a psychic person who is able to connect human beings (or so-called "living" people) with nonphysical (or so-called "dead") entities. Mediums, or channelers as they are also known, can contact those in spirit and transmit messages and information from the other side of the veil (see below). Some mediums pass along what is said or shown to them. Others, called trance mediums or trance channelers, go into an altered state of consciousness and do not alter what is being said. Trance mediums can put their consciousness temporarily aside and, like a telephone, allow the nonphysical entity to speak through them. Not all psychics are mediums, but all mediums are psychic.

The Mysterious Veil

The veil is an invisible barrier that separates the seen and unseen worlds. The permeability of this veil is directly affected by thought patterns, will, and belief. This so-called veil separating the human realm from the spirit world is growing thinner as the vibratory rate of our planet is being raised. This vibratory rate rises as mankind evolves and grows in spiritual understanding, for everything is basically energy. The dense, physical or material state is due to a very low frequency of energy vibration. If we raise our frequency, we more easily perceive the existence of higher vibratory rates, such as that of nonphysical beings. A primary way of raising our frequency is through meditation and prayer. When this happens, spirit communication becomes easier. Have you noticed how many psychic mediums are around? They're everywhere! Are they all genuine? Probably not all, and all your discrimination must be used to avoid being taken in by phonies. However, from my experience, there definitely are those who can contact and exchange messages with those in the nonphysical realm. One thing is certain, though: There has never been a greater interest or involvement in the subject of spirit work as there is now. This is good, because it will be easier for you as familiarity and acceptance of this field grows with people in general. We are only human and, therefore, are very much influenced by acceptance or resistance by others.

There is also increasingly less resistance from organized religions as more and more people seek to reconnect with their departed loved ones. Positive energy and support from fellow human beings contributes to the thinning of the veil.

When there is less resistance from nonbelievers and organized religion, fear decreases. As the fear factor declines, the spirit world is much more accessible to all those who reach out for spirit communication.

Most important of all is love. Love transcends fear and negativity. Your departed loved ones and spirit teachers lovingly and patiently wait for any contact with us. Universal laws are stringent and ensure that human beings are protected and not frightened, which is why much spirit contact occurs while we are sleeping.

Why oppose spirit connection, which when used with discrimination and pure intent, heals, regenerates the spirit, and mends a broken heart?

Can I Use This Technique
to Contact Departed Pets?

Yes, you can. Most people have a great desire to contact their beloved, loyal pets after their demise, just as we wish to communicate with the humans we have loved and lost. This technique can be used to communicate with animals as well as with people.

Beginning Connection

You can safely and easily begin connection yourself. As I said before, you don't have to go to a psychic, medium, tarot reader, or anyone else. All it takes is a few simple steps, a willingness, and the intent. Realize that communication may not happen with your first attempt. As with any worthwhile endeavor, success increases with the level of time, effort, and dedication invested. In Part II, the Seven Steps are presented so that they are as easy and effective as possible to use. Put them to work for you, using that which fits your belief system, and you will experience success.

Good luck! One thing is for sure: As you venture into the world of spirit communication, you will never see things quite the same way.

How to Begin

The following are intended as preliminary steps to opening the channels of communication not only with your departed loves, but also with your angels. As you will see, angels are an important step in the process. Angels are wonderful. They give us hope. They are waiting to be called upon. Amazingly, just about everyone believes in them. According to a recent poll on *Entertainment Tonight*, more than 90 percent of the population trusts in the existence of angels. Best of all, believing in them doesn't offend anyone. Angels will help just about anyone who requests their help. Their help, however, can be so subtle that we can miss it. In the Seven Steps I'll explain the ways we can communicate with angels so that your loved ones' messages are understood.

Sometimes the communication from the unseen world can be very delicate and almost impossible to discern. Angels and departed loved ones are all around us, and are waiting to help. Their service to mankind helps them grow in God's kingdom. They do, however, almost always have to be asked for help, and they have to be shown appreciation. We have to know and understand their rules.

Always ask as clearly as possible what you would like God and his angels to do for you. All prayers and requests are heard and evaluated, believe it or not! When we would like them to help us and they don't, it means that they have to step back to allow us to experience a certain lesson.

Angels are supportive, interactive beings of light and energy. Angels hear our prayers, but cannot respond without the go-ahead from the highest power, from God. If you want to see or communicate with angels for help with contacting departed loved ones, you have to keep asking. When your soul's growth allows it, it will happen.

There are many ways of reaching angels, and through them, loved ones. Of course, many of us have seen angels in times of crisis, emergency, or before the death experience. However, contacting spirit helpers while we are not in an emergency situation requires a bit more practice and effort.

Will You Settle for a Breeze in a Closed Room?

First of all, recognize the extremely high energy of angels. Angels are pure, high, electrical energy and have never been in a physical body. Spirit loved ones, of course, have been in a physical body and have a more hands-on, practical understanding of what you are requesting. The angels, however, are much more powerful and have virtual free reign over what they can and can't do for us . . . again, all in keeping with the higher plan for each person. All prayers and requests are received by angels, and are presented to the Creator for consideration.

Angels, do, however, make their presence known to us, usually in the most subtle of ways (unless it is an emergency). Angels or loved ones can make contact with a gentle breeze, or a brushing of air against the cheek, or one of their favorite ways—license plates! Yes, the most subtle messages are often delivered when we least expect it, such as on license plates while we're waiting for a traffic light.

Once a message on a license plate appeared for me when I had a particularly difficult decision to make. As I was waiting for the light to change I saw in front of me: GOFERIT. Messages also appear on billboards, and even in lotto numbers. If they look like your lucky numbers, recognize it, spend a dollar, and maybe you'll get lucky!

Of course, I know you are looking for concrete proof of communication. You don't want to hear about possible winning numbers, ripples in a pond, or leaves rustling when there is no breeze . . . or even an impression or outline left on a bed or a chair when you know that no one has been there. You don't want to hear about a tickling sensation on the skin, hair standing straight up, or gooseflesh. Or you don't want to hear about fragrances, like roses, that can't be explained.

What about a feeling of joy and euphoria that sweeps over you for no reason at all? What about animals or birds that come up to you and convey loving thoughts or messages? What about gifts from Spirit like a hankie, a feather, a beautiful stone, or a piece of jewelry, which seems to have mysteriously appeared? That's all fine, but you want more, right? You want solid spirit communication. Okay. In Part II, the Seven Steps will teach you how to achieve just that.

A Warning

As I'm sure you know, there are spirit entities in the universe that are downright malevolent. There are others that are playful and not necessarily harmful. They are probably just bored because they have not yet gone into God's highest light. In other words, they are temporarily stuck by their own desire to stay close to the physical plane instead of proceeding to a higher vibration where they can advance their development. These are usually spirits who like to play games. They love Ouija boards, because it gives them an avenue of expression, and alleviates their boredom. That is why we must always ask God, or the highest forces of good in the universe, to bring us only the highest and purest spirit energy.

Photograph of the author with the sinister figure in the window curtain over her head, while her son and brother are using the Ouija board. Cautions against using a Ouija board have merit. *(Photograph by Jack Keller)*

You don't want to be involved with spirits who are of low vibration. They are the ones who may be looking for an opportunity to swoop into a person's consciousness and create havoc. This interference can be in the form of encouraging humans to be involved in negative actions, words, or thoughts. These psychic bugs latch onto a physical being and influence behavior and thought. They are responsible for much in the world that is distressing, and can easily influence us when we are vulnerable. We are especially vulnerable to this form of spirit influence when we are tired, inebriated, weak, depressed, or under the influence of mind-altering drugs.

Unless you are an experienced medium, I strongly advise against the use of Ouija boards. Using a Ouija board is very much like having a big party, throwing open your front door, and allowing anyone to enter who wishes to join in. Unwittingly, you may invite in a dangerous spirit.

If we were "open" and able to see, hear, and receive all that is happening in the spirit world, we would probably go insane in a very short period of time. The separation between the physical and nonphysical is, for the most part, very busy, noisy, crowded, and often very loud. To say it's very much like Times Square on New Year's Eve at midnight is not far from the truth. That is why each of us in a physical body has a protective force known in the spirit world as a doorkeeper. It is up to that entity to protect us, and to not allow us to have any spirit contact that would be frightening or damaging to us. Our auric shield, aura, or energy field, which extends out from each of us for about a foot or so, also protects and insulates us. However, our doorkeeper and auric shield are not invincible. When we use alcohol, drugs, or anything that is mind-altering, our auric shield is easily torn and penetrated.

Unfortunately, I have had a few out-of-body experiences that were less than joyful. I've astrally projected during my sleep state to rather distressing places, such as prisoner-of-war camps. I went there, though, of my own accord, and prepared myself for the inherent difficulties. In the following chapters I will teach you how to protect yourself, and how your angels and spirit guides also protect you so that you do not experience anything negative or anything for which you don't *expressly* give permission.

Always Use Protection

I do have some caveats before you begin. Your energy has to be as pure and as high as possible to avoid attracting lower entities, psychic bugs, or attachments. The following steps will raise and purify your energy so as to create a hospitable environment for positive spirit communication.

To cleanse yourself and the area where you will be working:

- Burn Indian smudge and sandalwood incense. Wave the burning smudge particularly in the corners of the room where spirit entities love to gather. Corners of rooms are psychically powerful because this configuration allows energy to become concentrated. You may also spray holy water or Florida water around the room, particularly in the corners.

- Get rid of clutter. In addition to being physically confusing, clutter confuses the mental and spiritual states as well.

- Have a big glass of water nearby. Water is the universal purifier and is helpful in collecting negative energy.* Change the water daily. Throw it out, and never drink it!

- Do not smoke or use alcohol, as this attracts a low vibration of entities.

- Avoid coffee and other stimulants to help you get into a relaxed, serene state.

- Wear white, which is the purest form of energy. Wearing white helps to strengthen your aura.

- Play uplifting music. Sing a cheerful song, like "You Are My Sunshine."

- Read and recite something sacred, such as a passage from the Bible, Torah, or Koran. From the Bible I especially recommend Psalms.

---

*Water has always been recognized as a cleansing agent primarily on a physical level, as with human baths; however, it is also spiritually cleansing. Very simply, it raises a person's vibrations, even if they are only bathing in a tub. Water is a conductor of positive energy, while also being capable of drawing in and holding negative energy.

- When in meditation or prayer, do not cross anything on your body, like your feet, legs, arms, and hands. Crossing cuts the flow of energy that runs along the spiritual pathways of the body, called meridians. The exception to this is the yoga position known as the lotus, which I will discuss later.

Additional suggestions to help bring the right spirits to you:

- Have an absolutely quiet place set aside for your contact work, with no phones, light, or other interferences.

- Be relaxed and receptive.

- Accept what happens. Ridicule of any kind, even in your own mind, weakens the bond and may cause the loved one to refrain from contact.

- Pay attention to subtle messages. Contact generally begins in the most gentle, barely perceptible of ways.

- Collect photos and memorabilia that belonged to your departed loved ones and place them nearby.

- Let a tape recorder run in case you wish to make vocal notes, or enter an altered state and Spirit speaks through you. You may be surprised at what you find later.

- You will also want to manually record any impressions or messages that you receive. Have a paper and pencil ready for this purpose.

When you begin:

- Close your eyes. Breathe deeply. Say a prayer that asks for protection from God or the highest power in the universe. State that you welcome your angels and spirit loved ones who would like to communicate with you.

- Ask your spirit loved ones direct questions. Ask your spirit loved ones for a heavenly tour of their realm.

- Stretch your arms upward, with palms up and open. Do this with a feeling of love, and ask to receive their love and support. Love is the key to spirit contact and communication. Let your desire for communication come from your heart. Surround yourself with the full armor of God's love and protection.

In Part II you will learn specific centering and opening techniques to use in making contact. Time and patience will help you achieve results. If you have done this work in other lifetimes, you may surprise yourself with how quickly you receive a response. Part II will cover how to facilitate this contact in a gentle, easy, and protected way.

Over the years, many of my students have had amazing connection experiences. As they have used the techniques in this book they have raised their consciousness and their vibratory levels, and with this their ability to receive, understand, and perceive messages. Some of their experiences are included in this book.

Whatever happens, never forget the power of prayer. Ask to be surrounded in white light for protection. Express gratitude to God and his angels, your guides, and your doorkeeper for the assistance and support you receive.

Places for Contact

In addition to the suggestions outlined in the Seven Steps, in general any place where there is moving or still water is a prime spot for spirit contact. Also effective are natural settings like forests and glades; high places like mountains; thresholds of rooms; places where streams and bodies of water divide or come together; forks in roads; accident sites; or places where people are about to pass away into spirit, like hospitals. If you find yourself in one of these settings you may experience spontaneous connection. Spirits also love to congregate where there are joyful celebrations, singing, and laughing. They love to be where there are newborn babies. They tend to congregate in places of power like high-tension lines and power plants. Sacred places of worship always draw spirits and angels.

Spirits also congregate at natural power points on the earth, like Sedona, Arizona; Lourdes in France; Machu Picchu in Peru; Mount Shasta in California; Medjugorje in Yugoslavia; and many others. Tremendous power has been built up in places such as these from ongoing interaction of angels and human beings.

Now let's move on.

Invictus

Beyond this place of wrath and tears
Looms but the horror of the shade;
And yet the menace of the years
Finds, and shall find me unafraid.

—WILLIAM ERNEST HENLEY

TWO

Can You Experience
After-Death Communication?

Oh, my, it's very beautiful over there!

—THOMAS EDISON

Grieving the death of a loved one is one of the most intensely painful, traumatic experiences known to mankind. Death is an assault on our hearts, minds, and spirits. It deeply touches our souls. Unfortunately, it is an experience that we will all have to endure at some point in our lives, due to the simple fact that everyone dies.

The most difficult part of death, for most of us, is that we have to accept that our loved ones are permanently gone from our lives. We may never be able to communicate with them again, at least while we are still in a physical body. Nothing provokes deeper anguish and sadness than this thought.

After-death communication, or ADC, can help to alleviate that sadness. It occurs when our loved ones contact us directly after

they have passed on. An ADC is special because it is a spontaneous message or experience that comes without the assistance of
a psychic or a medium.

Science offers evidence of after-death communication. It is
believed that what we commonly call the "soul" is composed of
energy. If we remember what we learned in high school science,
that energy cannot be destroyed but merely changes form, it is only
logical that some aspect of human consciousness survives death.

As Dr. Melvin Morse, a leading near-death-experience researcher,
says, we all have the ability to communicate with loved ones after
death. After-death communication is thought by many researchers to
originate in the right temporal lobe of the brain. This is the same area
of the brain where the well-documented phenomenon of the near-
death experience is processed.

Have you ever sensed a presence? That's a great start. Have you ever
had a feeling that you were not alone? Have you ever had a vision? These
usually occur when we are very relaxed. They can be two-dimensional
and flat, or three-dimensional like a hologram. Visions are usually manifested in radiant colors, and may be seen either physically, or with your
mind's eye. Also important are your twilight experiences, which occur
as you are falling asleep, waking up, meditating, or praying.

Between 1988 and 1994, two thousand couples located in fifty
American states and the ten Canadian provinces were interviewed
about whether or not they had had ADC experiences. The results
indicated that 20 percent of the population claimed to have had at
least one of these experiences. This indicates that fifty million
Americans have personally experienced contact at least once.
These were spontaneous ADC experiences, with no involvement
with psychics, mediums, hypnotists, or devices of any kind.

Some very notable figures throughout history have reported having ADC experiences. Cicero, the ancient Roman philosopher and
writer, wrote an essay on ADC called "On Divination." Robert Burton,
a sixteenth-century English scholar, described ADC incidents in his
time period in his writings. Thomas Edison, Napoléon Bonaparte,
Benjamin Franklin, author C. S. Lewis, and Gen. George S. Patton also
wrote about spirit communication. In the case of Edison, he heard the

voice of his late assistant, Mr. Lemming, speaking to him when he was working on an early model of his dictating machine.

Types of ADC

Communication with our departed loved ones may happen at any time and any place, and may in fact already be occurring. As you embark on your journey toward making contact, know that communication is a two-way street. ADC may already be occurring and may, in fact, be taking any variety of forms.

While contact can be brought about through direct request and through the processes found in the next section, communication may not necessarily be as direct as you would expect—at first.

There are many types of ADCs. Perhaps your loved ones will visit you and you will see them quite clearly, as if you could reach out and touch them. On other occasions, you may see a transparent apparition. These are visual ADCs.

These apparitions often manifest in the corners of rooms. Sometimes you are able to see them with the physical eye, other times you will perceive something from the corner of your eye, but when you turn to see it more clearly, it will not be there. This can happen when you're at home, at work, grocery shopping, or anywhere at all. Many apparitions appear bedside, or at the foot of beds. Very often, these apparitions smile or just wave. With practice, visual encounters can turn into verbal communication. Many of these verbal visitations occur during meditation or while we are in a relaxed state.

One of my listeners, William, reported waking up at 3 A.M. and seeing a hazy outline of his departed brother John at the foot of his bed. After a few moments, William intuitively received the message, "Tell Timmy that I love him." Timmy is John's son, and he missed his father terribly. William's brother then faded away.

Have you have you ever felt or sensed a presence? You may have thought that you were imagining things. However, this feeling, or knowing that a departed loved one is near is often real. It can happen shortly after the passing of someone or years afterward. This is called sentient ADC.

For instance, before my children were told that their grandmother had passed away, she came to them in a very sweet, nonfrightening way to say good-bye. She appeared smiling in the window of their bedrooms, directly in front of their beds.

An aural ADC experience is when you actually hear a departed loved one speak to you. It could be just one word. Sometimes it may feel as if you are talking to someone who is still in the physical body. While most common aural ADCs are telepathic communications, they may occur in a variety of ways.

Virginia, one of my radio listeners, reported that during the week after her mother passed away, her phone rang. When she picked up the phone, she heard a faint voice that said, "Ginny, this is mother. I miss you and love you. Thank you, thank you for everything." Before Virginia could gain her composure, she heard a click.

Sometimes after a loved one passes away, the phone will ring. Perhaps it will ring at a time when the departed one usually called while still in the physical body. For instance, many parents call their grown children before they go to sleep at night, say at eleven o'clock. After their passing, the phone will ring at that same time, but there won't be anyone on the line. It's not always easy or possible to vocally express oneself without a body. Under certain conditions, however, it is possible.

Occasionally you may actually feel a spirit touch you. This tangible ADC can manifest as a touch on your hand, a kiss on your cheek, a gentle hug, or a rub on your shoulders. Tangible ADCs come in when your loved one wants to comfort you by touching you. A listener, Joan, was sleeping in her departed mother's bed when she awoke to the familiar, loving stroke of her mother's hand on her forehead.

Fragrant ADC is when you smell your departed loved one. Perhaps it might be the smell of a cigar, pipe, cigarette, perfume, or cologne. The scent is distinctively representative of your loved one. It seems to be easiest for our spirit loved ones to surround us with the smell of flowers, particularly roses, which have a strong scent. Many people smell flowers when driving in a car with closed windows. This is always a wonderful spirit greeting. When Alice, who had read my *Calling All Angels* book, was driving in a closed car on a cold winter day, she suddenly noticed the beautiful smell of roses in her car. Roses were her deceased mother's favorite fragrance. She knew that it was a warm, wonderful greeting from her mom.

Sometimes a departed loved one can come to us in the form of a little bird, or even a gentle butterfly. Don't disregard this ADC, known as symbolism. My mother had always felt that dead birds were bad luck. When we returned from her funeral, a dead bird was lying on her doormat.

Did you ever find a coin whose appearance couldn't be explained, or flashes of light in a dark room? Have you ever had your television turn itself on? This is quite possibly phenomena ADC from your spirit world. Sometimes lightbulbs will flicker. I remember sitting in the funeral home with my family as we made preparations after my mother's passing. The lightbulb on the undertaker's desk would not stop flickering. I asked the undertaker if that was a normal occurrence. As I suspected, he said that it wasn't.

Perhaps you have experienced the following kinds of ADC:

- visually seen departed loved ones

- heard them, possibly doing similar things as they did in the physical body, like working in the kitchen and rattling dishes

- smelled scents

- received spirit gifts or tokens

- had chills or goose bumps for no apparent reason

- felt a gentle touch or a hug

- experienced visions or dreams

- undergone electrical problems, like bulbs that flicker or burn out too soon

- felt lost in time, a warped sense of time

- noticed indentations or impressions in furniture, with an unseen presence

- experienced photographic fogginess and images
- noted movement or disappearance of items
- received mysterious phone calls
- became aware of movement of heavy or light objects, like chairs
- undergone synchronicity, or coinciding contact from people you were just thinking about
- discerned the blinking of small balls or flashes of light close to your head
- detected a presence to the side of your line of vision, yet when you turned to look, it seemed as if nothing was there

While you may not have known it at the time, these may very well have been manifestations of spirit and greetings of love and support.

ADC is generally spontaneous, may occur at any time and under any situation, and is usually a surprise. It is often accompanied by a message that needs to be received.

Sometimes departing loved ones just give a little smile or wave, in a very gentle, nonthreatening way. Other times before falling asleep, when we're in that half-awake, half-asleep state, we experience "hypnogogic" hallucinations, as they are scientifically called. These are actual encounters with people we have loved and lost. These experiences can occur when we are not thinking about the loved one or can be of a person we don't recognize. It's usually a face or series of faces that seem to float in our consciousness during that last fleeting moment before we fall asleep. With some effort, we can train ourselves to gently maintain that nebulous state for a period of several seconds or even longer.

A client, Janet, was very tired and fell into a light sleep state while she was driving alone. She was quickly and abruptly awakened, though, when someone tugged strongly on her hair and said, "Janna, wake up." Her mother used to call her Janna.

Here are some common situations during which spontaneous after-death communication can occur:

- During dreams. This is probably the most common type.
- During prayer, meditation, or reverie.
- While under anesthesia.
- During near-death experience (NDE).
- During great trauma, like accidents, emergencies, war, personal crisis, weather calamities, fear, shock, high fever, and serious illness.
- While experiencing physical or spiritual healing.
- From a loved one who has recently completed the death transition, and who wishes to lovingly "touch-in."
- When working with electrical devices, such as tape recorders.
- Through automatic writing. It's as if the handwriting is not yours, but someone else's.
- When holding a seashell against the ear.
- At spirit circles, also known as séances.
- Through the use of techniques outlined in this book.

Some people seem more adept at ADC. These individuals often include:

- Young children, many of whom tell their parents of contact they have had with deceased relatives, often their grandparents.
- Surviving children of multiple births who have experienced the loss of their deceased siblings.
- Members of the clergy.

- Someone who is in the process of passing away and who wishes to say farewell.

Our challenge in attempting ADC is that it involves an area of the brain that we rarely use. As such, we're not adept at using it to send or receive messages from those who are deceased. This is the part of the brain that this book seeks to develop.

Out-of-Body Travel

Sometimes out-of-body ADCs occur while we are asleep or in a meditative state. These out-of-body ADCs involve leaving the body and visiting your departed loved one where he or she exists. These experiences can be more vivid than life and are usually filled with love and joy.

Janice, a regular listener, reported being taken on a visit by her daughter, Sara, who had passed away several years previously. Sara took Janice to a lovely garden by a beautiful river and said that this was where she was staying.

Another listener, Sam, whose mother had recently passed on, was taken to a classroom by a robed figure, who identified himself as Elijah. This was a classroom just like on earth, Elijah pointed out, and Sam's mother was learning about where she was.

Automatic Handwriting

Many people find success with automatic handwriting, a form of channeling in which you sit quietly in meditation with paper and pen or pencil in hand. After a while, your hand may start to write as if it were being controlled by someone else. A typewriter or computer may also be used. Entire volumes have been written this way by authors like Ruth Montgomery (*A Search for Truth*) and Neale Donald Walsch (*Conversations with God*).

Automatic handwriting can often start during our sleep hours. We may be awakened with a strong desire to write down what we have received while asleep. Most people probably do a form of automatic handwriting while awake, especially when it's practiced on a daily basis. The after-death communication that expresses itself through handwriting may be written in a script that is quite different from your actual handwriting. If you feel like trying ADC automatic handwriting, sit quietly and close your eyes. When you feel inspired to write, maybe a word, maybe a *whole book*, start writing. You may be amazed, and find that you have received paranormal information such as predictions, advice, or messages of love and devotion. There will be more about automatic handwriting in Part II.

Preparation for ADC

Most ADCs are positive, joyful and uplifting encounters that take away grief. They provide lasting comfort, support, and hope, while accelerating emotional and spiritual healing. The biggest hurdle, however, is overcoming the fear that has a way of acting as a wall between us and the spirit world.

You are normal if you experience fear because ADC is a new experience for you. If you are startled by the suddenness of the experience, or are afraid that you are losing your mind, try to relax. Realize that this is a normal reaction. The more you read about ADC and familiarize yourself with the phenomenon, the more comfortable it will seem to you. Give yourself time. Know that God loves you, and that God and his angels protect you while surrounding you with universal love. ADC is a natural part of life.

The more you use meditation and prayer, the more comfortable you will be with ADC. It's important to believe and remember that ADC experiences always expand one's understanding of life. With that understanding comes a deeper, more profound awareness of life after death. The more you know and experience, the less afraid you will be.

All this is nice, you may say, but what do you do with this information? How do you actually communicate with your missing loved ones by drawing on what you've learned and assimilating contact into your lifestyle in a straightforward, easy way?

Please understand that this information has been relayed in order to give you choices and understanding. We all operate under free will. A suggestion that may be correct for one person may not be right for another. You may wish to incorporate yogic breathing and positions into your connection practice, or you may wish to use your own exercises. You may like the idea of a spirit space, but feel that it is impractical and will, instead, set up a simple altar in the corner of your home. You may believe in God but not in this particular name for God, and you may have prayers other than the ones suggested here that you will wish to use. You may have selected those affirmations that have particular relevance for you. This is all fine. The idea is to give you choices and to relate what I have found to be essential, and what works for most people.

Part II teaches formal steps to open the lines of communication and clear the way for ADC. Put it all together for a transcendent, life-long journey of communication with those angels and guides who are working with you and reaching those who have departed.

I'll leave you with this thought:

Ellie reported that as she was driving through a heavy thunderstorm, she drove through a deep puddle and the car spun out of control. She was about to have a head-on collision with another car. Terrified, she realized that she could do nothing to prevent an accident and said a quick prayer. Suddenly, an unseen hand seemed to exert a superhuman force and pulled the wheel away from the oncoming car. In addition, it looked as if a huge wall of water had been created. There was extra insulation and protection for both drivers. Moments later, Ellie's car was filled with the fragrance of gardenias, her mother's favorite flower.

As it says in one holy book:

Ask and it shall be given to you;
Seek and you shall find;
Knock and it shall be opened to you
—MATT. 7:7

PART II

Contact Your Loved Ones in Seven Easy Steps

In steps one through seven,
We will connect earth and heaven.

—JOYCE KELLER

THREE

Step One:
Call on Your Angels
and Spirit Teachers

It is not known precisely where angels dwell,

whether in the air, the void or the planets.

It has not been God's pleasure that we

should be informed of the abode.

—Voltaire

The universe can be a tricky place to navigate by oneself. As worlds connect, angels, and also your spirit guides, offer that extra edge of protection and guidance. Angels are part of all spirit communication, whether it is requested or not. However, requesting their assistance will raise the vibrations and strengthen communication.

The following are the nine bands, or types, of angels and their responsibilities:

1. Seraphim: The angels of love.

2. Cherubim: The angels of wisdom.

3. The Thrones: The angels who oversee the other angels.

4. The Dominions: The angels of mercy.

5. The Virtues: The angels of miracles.

6. The Powers: The angels who guide souls.

7. The Principalities: The angels who guide nations.

8. The Archangels: The angels of spiritual tasks.

9. The Angels: The angels who intercede between God and humans.

How Do We Know When Angels Are Around Us?

Angels have a subtle energy, so you must make a concerted effort to be aware of things that most people miss.

A feather that drifts down and lands in front of your feet, a message that appears on a car's license plate—there are so many ways that angels interact with us. Once you start paying attention, you will be amazed and amused at what you observe. The secret to understanding how angels connect the physical and nonphysical worlds is to pay attention, especially when enjoying the beauties of nature.

When Can Angels Connect Us
with Our Departed Loved Ones?

The strongest angelic activity seems to be at the start and the end of each day, at dawn and at dusk. These are also the most natural times for meditation. The next best times are noon and midnight. The times of seasonal changes are also powerfully angelic.

Other times may be during frightening thunderstorms, or times of gentle, warm rain, or during times that snow has just fallen on the ground and is white and pristine. No wonder so many of us have played the game "angels in the snow."

For months, Ellen had been asking her angels to help her contact her deceased baby. Finally, as Ellen drifted off into sleep on her porch one evening, the little girl came to her. The child told her to stop grieving. She said, "Mom, don't be sad anymore! Have another baby. I'll be it! I love you, Mamma!"

Ellen said she felt as if the sun had suddenly come out.

Angelic energy can be strongly felt when we are on swings or hammocks, or when we are gazing in mirrors while in a dark room. It is also possible to feel the presence of angels or see them in the sky when we watch the movements of clouds.

Where Are the Best Places for
Angels to Help Us Connect?

Primarily, these are places with is moving water and in natural settings, such as forests and glades. Also powerful are very high places, and places with clean air, such as mountains and tall hills. Thresholds of rooms are power spots, as are corners of rooms. In front of fireplaces and in your bed, especially before you fall asleep or when you first awaken, are powerful spots, too. Believe it or not, your table where you eat is powerful, especially if you set a space aside from time to time for your angels.

Places of spirit connection are also potent where streams and bodies of water divide, forks in the road, and accident sites, especially if that is where your loved one crossed over. Angels also support and help our spirit communication at places where people are about to pass away, such as hospitals.

Mark was praying over the body of his father in his hospital room, when he felt a strong presence. Looking up he saw the soft outline of a male angel. Words came into his head without realizing it: "Your father wants you to be happy for him, for he is no longer in pain." Mark then got the word that his father would speak to him directly, as soon as he was able.

Create an Inner and Outer Altar

A physical altar creates a powerful angelic atmosphere. It is an attraction for energy on both sides of the veil. It can be created very easily in a small, private area of your home. Corners are particularly attractive to spirit energy. There is almost always a buildup of power in corners of rooms. Ideally, you should use a small table covered by a white cloth, as white represents the purest from of energy. Any pure white cloth will do: a pillowcase, a handkerchief, or an inexpensive piece of cloth from the fabric store. Place a photo on the altar of the spirit you would like to contact. If you wish, add a picture of a spiritual teacher such as Jesus or Moses. Leave open a Bible, Torah, Koran, or other holy book. Include a bowl of water, since water is a great conductor of spiritual energy. Pour the water out after your communication sessions. Talismans, artifacts, religious medals, and relics might be added.

Add a white candle in a sturdy, fireproof holder. White is the highest vibration and will make your spirit communication smoother.

Write the departed loved ones' name on a piece of paper, and place it on the altar. Adding fresh flowers is always a nice touch.

The best, most effective altar is an invisible one, however, that you create within you. This is an altar that you create in your imagination. It is your own, unseen private, personal sanctuary. You will visualize it in your mind's eye. You will always be comfortable, safe, and protected there. No one can invade it.

You can visualize a church, temple, mountain retreat, or place in nature. It's up to you. After you have created it and can see it clearly, send positive energy to your sanctuary. It will become crystallized or set in your heart, mind, and spirit. No one can take it away from you; no one can go there without an invitation from you. Each time you use it as a private, personal sanctuary, it will be strengthened and empowered by your commitment. Your invisible altar is a point in the heart and mind where there is a thinning of the veil between the two dimensions. It is a place where those in spirit can approach you on your own terms, and with equally open hearts. There is no fear! The more you develop it in your mind, the stronger your own spirit link will grow.

Another beautiful feature of your own personal inner sanctuary is that you can make minor or major adjustments, all in keeping with your soul's growth and desires.

Your inner altar is a place where the seen and unseen, or the real and unreal, come together.

You must give your permission before any spirit loved ones can enter your sanctuary. Ignore any irritating thoughts about the fact that it might all be in your imagination. Ask your spirit teachers to give you clarity, truth, understanding, and comfort. It is their job to do this for you. At your request, they will comply.

What Angels Love

In addition to altars, angels also love bells, chimes, or anything that rings with a beautiful or pleasant sound. The delicate tones of a small handheld bell, or even the gentle tinkling of the bell on a cat's collar, will assist angels in their efforts on your behalf. Wind chimes also attract spirit loved ones. A quick way of attracting angels is to ring a small bell, a couple of times. It quickly draws angels and spirit loved ones close to you.

Primarily, angels love when you radiate peace and tranquillity. As Yogananda said, "If you keep your mind on the resolve to never lose your peace, then you can attain Godliness. Keep a secret chamber of silence within yourself, where you will not let moods, trials, battles, or disharmony enter. Keep out all hatred, revengeful feelings, and excessive desires. In this chamber of peace, God and His angels will assist you."

Once when I was in a deep state of meditation, a beautiful angel with long, blonde, flowing hair appeared to me and started speaking. "Joyce, do you remember when you were eight years old, and almost drowned in Southampton Lake?"

I whispered, "Oh, yes. I've never been quite the same around water."

This lovely angel continued, "Well, I came into your being, and into your consciousness at that time. I came from a very great distance to be with you."

"You entered my consciousness during the time I was drowning?"

"Yes, when you had that moment when things went black . . . that's when I came in. Right before George rescued you."

George was my cousin, who died some years after this incident.

I answered, "I'm happy to have you, of course, but why are you with me?"

She softly replied, "George wants to send his best to you." She smiled, and slowly faded away. She appeared again, years later, to inspire me, and to help me write my book *Calling All Angels*.

How Else Can Angels Help Us to Communicate?

Take a walk at the beach. Choose a beautiful conch or seashell. Hold it up to your ear, after asking your angels to connect you with your loved one. You may not hear anything initially, but eventually you will. Don't laugh, but this also works with a disconnected telephone! Angels love to make us happy. If they can do something to make us smile, they will do it.

When using the shell or disconnected telephone, at first you may hear nothing. It may take some time, practice, and effort. At some point, you may hear something. Perhaps only a very high, barely perceptible beep or two, or perhaps a whisper, hum, or the sound of rolling thunder. If you cannot understand what you hear, express this in words to your angels and spirit teachers. Ask that the message be brought to your correct auditory level. It's all a matter of faith, adjustment, and fine-tuning. The point is, if you're calling the spirit world, sooner or later your spirit loved ones will answer you.

How Can You Call on Your Own Angel to Help?

There are a variety of ways in which we can call out to our angels. You may try using these prayers, remembering to first physically and spiritually cleanse yourself and your environment as much as possible.

Use this prayer for help with connection:

Angel Prayer for Use in Spirit Connection
Angel of God, my guardian dear
To whom God's love commits me here,
Ever this day be at my side
To light, to guard, to rule, to guide.

Use this prayer to ask for protection:

For Angelic Protection
Guardian angel
Protect me with your might
When connecting with spirit
Both day and night.

I recommend the following:

1. Begin with one or both prayers above. Request protection for yourself or others involved with the prayer request.

2. State the appropriate affirmation that follows, in keeping with your birth sign.
3. In meditation, visualize beams of white light coming down from angelic worlds and surrounding you. The white light permeates every cell of your being.
4. Have the attitude of receptivity, strength, power, and appreciation for the angelic assistance offered.
5. Your atmosphere will have higher vibrations and energy if incense is burned. Add fresh flowers and a glass of water.
6. If you wish to use aromatherapy, you may want to use angelica, cassis, or sunlily in combination or alone.
7. Use one of the tools listed later in this chapter (see "Tools to Connect with Your Angels").
8. Express gratitude.

The following rhyme is helpful for expressing gratitude to angels after they have assisted you with spirit communication:

For Angelic Appreciation
Heavenly angels
Thank you for all!
You helped, you heard
You answered my call.

*Make friends with the angels who though invisible
are always with you . . . often invoke them, constantly
praise them, and make good use of their help and
assistance in all of your temporal and spiritual affairs.*
—St. Francis de Sales,
French churchman

Angel-Assisted Spirit Communication
by Birth Sign

Each sign of the zodiac has its own angel. That angel will work with you and help you to communicate with your departed loved ones if asked directly.

The following verses and affirmations may be repeated throughout the day and before meditation. Repeat the rhyme and affirmation for your birth sign, and if you know it, the rhyme and affirmation for the person you would like to contact.

> **Aries:** *SARIEL is your Aries Angel*
> *March 21–April 19*
> Sariel, Aries angel,
> Protector of my head,
> Connect me with spirit
> For words left unsaid.

Sariel, your special Aries angel, means "at God's command." When called upon, he will always make his presence or interaction known in the most positive, helpful way. He often manifests his energy with bright flashes of red lights or streaks.

The affirmation for Aries spirit connection is: "I know all will be well in my world. I will let go and let God."

> **Taurus:** *ANAEL is your Taurean angel*
> *April 20–May 20*
> Anael, Taurus angel,
> Protector of my neck,
> Connect me with spirit
> Keep all in check.

Anael, chief of the order of angels known as "principalities," and one of the seven angels of the creation, exercises dominion over the planet Venus, the planet of love, and also the ruling planet of Taurus.

The affirmation for Taurean spirit connection is: "I will not worry about money or security. I know the universe will amply provide for me."

> Gemini: *RAPHAEL is your Gemini angel*
> *May 21–June 21*
> Raphael, Gemini angel
> Protect my lungs and chest
> When it comes to connecting,
> You're the best!

Your connecting angel, Raphael, is known in heavenly realms as "the shining angel." When Raphael manifests, he may be seen with a staff and sandals, a water container, and a small wallet strapped over his shoulder. When it comes to any angels, don't necessarily look for wings or a halo. You may be disappointed!

Your affirmation for Gemini spirit connection is: "Staying awake will not accomplish anything. I will be happiest and most productive if I give up all worries and concerns. I will let God and my angel, Raphael, carry my worries away. I will fall into the deepest, most natural sleep. I will wake up feeling completely refreshed and well."

> Cancer: *GABRIEL is your Cancer angel*
> *June 22–July 22*
> Gabriel, my Cancerian angel,
> Protect me night and day
> When connecting with spirit
> Light and guide my way.

Gabriel, your Cancerian angel, is one of the four archangels named in Hebrew tradition and is considered one of the two highest-ranking angels in Judeo-Christian and Islamic religious lore.

The affirmation for Cancerian spirit connection is: "I have no reason to fear life, or to have feelings of lack of control over my life. I will no longer be concerned about anything, without just cause. My trust in God and my angels increases with each passing day."

> **Leo: *MICHAEL is your Leo angel***
> ***July 23–August 22***
> Michael, Leo angel
> Never fainthearted
> Connect me with loved ones
> Who are departed.

Michael, your Leo angel, ranks as the greatest angel in major religions. His name means, "who is of God," and he is the chief of the archangels, and the conqueror of Satan.

He acknowledges your need for perfection and your uncompromising standards. This is very commendable of course, unless it takes a toll on your physical well-being.

Your affirmation for Leo spirit connection is: "I don't have to spend my entire life doing things for other people. I can do what make me happy as well. I will find great joy in my life every day."

> **Virgo: *CHAMAEL is your Virgo angel***
> ***August 23–September 22***
> Chamael, Virgo angel,
> From realms above
> Help me connect
> To departed ones I love.

Chamael, your Virgo angel, is one of the seven archangels who not only help to protect health, but also do amazing spirit connection work. This wonderful angel also protects human beings from violence and war.

Your affirmation for Virgo spirit connection is: "I know that God and my angels will never let me down. They will always be there for me."

Libra: *JEHOEL is your Libran angel*
September 23–October 23
Jehoel, Libran angel
Don't let me fail
I miss my loved one
Please part the veil.

Jehoel, also known as Jehuel, your Libran angel of beauty and power, is represented by the scales of justice. Jehoel is the chief· of the angelic order of the seraphim. Jehoel is also the heavenly choirmaster who accompanied Abraham on his visit to paradise.

Your affirmation for Libran spirit connection is: "I am not afraid to experience joy. I am a child of God. God created me and wants me to be filled with the greatest happiness and fulfillment possible."

Scorpio: *METATRON is your Scorpion angel*
October 24–November 21
Metatron, Scorpion angel
Set my spirit free
Help me spiritually communicate
Let my third eye see.

"Metatron" is the name of the angel believed to be "one who sits closest to God." He also records the deeds of the soul, namely, the Akashic record. Metatron is considered to be one of the most powerful, loving angels in the universe.

Your affirmation for Scorpion spirit connection is: "I am living in the moment, listening carefully to that still, small, loving voice within. I have no time or patience for unworthy thoughts about sadness or disappointment from my past. I am moving forward in my life with great joy."

Sagittarius: *SACHIEL is your Sagittarian angel*
November 22–December 21:
Sachiel, Sagittarian angel

Protector of legs and hips
Connect my spirit world
To my eyes, ears, and lips.

Sachiel is an amazing angel who is one of the primary forces in
the order of angels known as cherubim. He will always encourage
you to express joy and happiness. This is one of his primary tools
when working with you in spirit communication.

Your affirmation for Sagittarian spirit connection is: "I understand and accept that in the deepest levels of my consciousness,
there are no barriers between the seen and the unseen worlds. I
open my heart, mind, and soul to the glories that await me, as I
connect to the loved ones on the other side of the veil."

Capricorn: CASSIEL is your Capricorn angel
December 22–January 19
Cassiel, Capricorn angel
Protector of knees
Connect me with spirit
With safety and ease.

Cassiel, which means "chosen by God," soars in the heavenly realm
as easily as he manifests as a homeless person on earth. Cassiel
salutes your winning and powerful personality. If you are a true
Capricorn workaholic, put your work and goals aside for a while
and work harder at tuning in to your spirituality.

Your affirmation for Capricorn spirit connection is: "I am not
afraid to change my mind and to see things from a different
prospective. I move ahead in my life with clarity and ease."

Aquarius: URIEL is your Aquarian angel
January 20–February 18
Uriel, Aquarian angel
Protector of ankles and calves
Connects me with spirit
With jovial laughs.

Uriel means "highest fire of God." This powerful angel has always been recognized as a cherub who stands at the gate of Eden, with a fiery sword, protecting his charges with thunder and bolts of lightning. He also rules with a great sense of humor and a sense of frivolity.

Your affirmation for Aquarius is: "I walk fearlessly and with humor through life. I recognize which problems are mine, and which ones are not. I will do all that I can to help others. I will be realistic in my expectations."

Pisces: *SANDALPHON is your Piscean angel*
February 19–March 20
Sandalphon, Piscean angel
Protector of toes and feet
Part the veil
For loved ones so sweet.

Sandelphon is a gloriously powerful angel who brings this primary message from the world of spirit: "The light of God will connect you to unseen worlds. Know that the unseen is as close as your breath."

Your affirmation for Piscean spirit connection is: "I have great control over my life and spirit connection. I cannot act like a sponge, though, and absorb the problems of others. I am at peace. I am tranquil and loving. I am a child of God. I know that God loves and protects me."

Angels may be very excellent sort of folk
in their own way, but we, poor mortals
in our present state, would probably
find them precious company
—JEROME K. JEROME

Tools to Connect with Your Angels

As a general rule, laugh as much as possible. Know that when you laugh, the aging process stops completely, the body heals, and spirit communication becomes easier. Spirits are uplifted through laughter and the feeling of optimism that accompanies it, and this raises your vibration, lowers your guard, and makes it easier for angels to connect with you. With this in mind, talk to a good friend, watch a funny movie, read a hilarious book, or do whatever it takes to raise your spirits high.

In addition to this and the recommendations already offered, consider one or more of the following to help facilitate spirit communication.

Crystals and Gems

Crystals, gems, and certain minerals are also tools that angels use to connect with spirit loved ones. The most helpful crystal is a plain quartz crystal. By plain, we mean quartz crystal, not the lower-vibration lead crystal. Lead crystal should never be used to connect spirit worlds, for it is not able to contain the energies from higher worlds. Other helpful crystals for connection to the spirit world are fluorite, moldavite, or tourmaline.

All crystals should be cleansed before using by leaving on a sunny windowsill for three days. The crystal should be "programmed" with your voice. Simply speak to it, and tell it what its purpose is. Your crystals or gems should be held in your hand, or placed casually in the area where spirit communication is being attempted.

Magnets

Many angels work powerfully with humans when magnets are used for spirit communication. Magnets represent the power of the earth, and its connection to the universe. Magnets were used in ancient LeMuria and Atlantis and have incredible energy. (LeMuria existed at roughly the same time as Atlantis, and these neighboring continents used magnets, as well as crystals, as a potent source of energy. Purportedly, it was the misuse of these and other powers that brought down the civilizations.) Magnetic power can be misused if not understood.

Magnets can enhance spirit communication when you have a basic understanding of their power and energy. Their polarity must be understood. The direction of the magnets is the secret of their success in spirit communication.

Meditating with magnets can be phenomenal. When the magnet points toward the north pole, or with the green tip, doors to spirituality can be safely opened. This is not the case, however, when the magnet points to the south pole, or with the orange tip. The magnet (or magnets) should simply be placed at the site of meditation, or wherever spirit communication is desired.

Magnetic jewelry is often a great spirit connector and can be used in meditation. A compass can also be placed on the meditation table or altar. Magnetic strips can be bought in any hardware store or hardware department and placed inside your shoes, sticky side pressed against the shoe, of course. This is great for walking meditation and spirit communication.

Magnets can also be placed at the head of your bed, but only if the head of the bed faces north, for maximum spirit communication. Warning: You may wake up very tired!

Pyramid Power

You may wish to create a simple pyramid to meditate under. The ancient Egyptians understood the magical power of the pyramid. They were used as temples, primarily because of their phenomenal ability to connect worlds. Angels are drawn to the concentrated energy created by pyramids.

My husband, Jack, used his pyramid, which he made from cardboard and strung over his favorite chair, to meditate under. He did this as an experiment and found that his meditations were more profound and powerful than usual.

Making a pyramid is very easy. You can use simple wire or bend open a wire hanger to the proper configuration. You might even wish to create a pyramid out of inexpensive materials, such as cardboard or balsa wood. Perhaps you'd like one that is big enough for you to sit in. Your spirit-connecting meditation will be enhanced. The key to success in working with pyramid energy, though, is the configuration. Ideally it should be of the same proportions as the Great Pyramid of Giza. Every great pyramid has precisely the same formula for its dimensions. That basic formula for a pyramid is: four equal sides, 1.57 × the height, made of four equilateral triangles. (Equilateral means that all three sides are the same length.)

You may sit under a pyramid to recharge your batteries, meditate, and more easily connect. Many people sleep under pyramids.

Music

Music truly is the language of the soul. If you were to hear a band of angels, beautiful music would likely be playing. Music is a vehicle for spirit travel. When spirit communication is desired, it is often arranged by angels via music. You don't have to play an instrument, sing, play a music CD, or do anything. It is enough to be aware that music is an integral part of the connection.

That is not to say, however, that you should not play music when attempting to work with angels. It's just the opposite! Angels speak to you clearly when you are listening to music, particularly soft, soothing, gentle music.

Robert was listening to his favorite tape, "Beethoven's Fifth Symphony in C Minor," when suddenly the tape went silent for a moment. He distinctly heard a voice that identified himself as Archangel Michael. He couldn't believe his ears. Then he heard the voice of his son, who had passed away in a car accident several months prior, say, "Dad, I love you!"

Sometimes it can be just the melody itself that encourages the connection between worlds. Usually, though, the lyrics are a very reliable way of calling angels to you. Listen carefully to lyrics. There are many, many hidden angelic messages in music. A perfect example of hidden spirit messages can be found in the song "Magic," by Olivia Newton-John, which sounds like it came directly from the spirit world.

Positive Thinking

As the great prophet Edgar Cayce said, "Attitude is everything." This is particularly true when attempting spirit communication. No negative thoughts! No expressions of unreasonable fears! Remember, fear equals absence of God. There is nothing wrong with attempting to connect the physical and nonphysical worlds. It is therapeutic to all concerned. Please keep in mind, though, no drugs, no alcohol. No negative people. No negative thoughts. Don't set up "don't" or "can't" barriers. They are very difficult to overcome. You are a child of God, so why not expect only positive spirit-connection experiences?

When Jill lost her beloved cat, "Mr. Charming," she was beyond consolation. He was an amazing cat, who had taken on the personality of a charming, endearing partner. Losing this cat was especially traumatizing to Jill, for within a six-month period, Jill had gone through a difficult divorce and lost her mother. She had barely recovered from these losses, when "Mr. C," as she called him, disappeared.

Jill tirelessly searched animal pounds, drove around many neighborhoods, and ran numerous photo ads. Nothing worked. Mr. C was nowhere to be found.

When she called in to the show, I didn't want to tell her what I was feeling. I didn't think that Mr. C was still in a physical body. I said to her, "Jill, ask your angels to tell you where Mr. C is, or ask him to speak to you himself!"

She said, "I don't think I can do that."

Of course, I said, "Give it a try. Maybe you'll be surprised."

The following show, Jill called in. "Guess what, Joyce? I asked my angels to see Mr. C. He came to me in a dream and said, 'Mommy, don't worry about me. Look! I can chase all the mice I want! I eat tuna all day. Please don't be sad!'" She added, "And, you know what else? I felt him purring and leaning on me, just like he always did."

She closed by saying, "He said he would visit me as often as possible."

I said, "Jill, enjoy that warm, purry spot. I'll tell you this, though, if you don't know it already, he wants you to get another cat!"

She said, "That's so funny, Joyce. He told me that, too!"

The Magical Connecting Power of Yoga

The world *yoga* means union—union with God and the divine world of spirit. We are referring to hatha yoga, or the yoga of physical postures and breath control. Hatha yoga consists of fifty-four primary postures known as "asanas." In combination with the breathing techniques known as "pranayama," this method has proven for more than six thousand years to be able to balance and harmonize the body, mind, and spirit. It is capable of bringing about outstanding spirit contact and alignment with your angels.

As the energies of the body are balanced through the yoga postures and yogic meditation, your angels, and likewise your spirit teachers, strengthen their spiritual bond with you.

The breathing techniques are vital, because breath, the essence of life, connects the mind and body to the highest spirit worlds. The breathing technique that is the stepping-off point to spirit connection is "The Complete Breath." It is contained in the following steps. With gently closed eyelids:

1. Sit in a relaxed position, on the floor or in a chair, with a straight spine. (A straight spine allows a better flow of energy from the base of the spine to the top of the head.)
2. Exhale completely. Inhale through your nose for five slow counts, as you fill the lower part of your lungs.
3. Continue inhaling for another five counts.
4. Hold for the count of five.
5. Exhale through your nose the upper part of your lungs for five.
6. Continue exhaling for another count of five. Squeeze out of your nose any remaining air in your lungs.
7. Breathe normally, keeping your eyes closed.
8. With your eyes still closed, roll your neck gently to

the right, all the way around. Repeat in the opposite
direction.

9. Stand, and drop gently forward into a position known
as "The Cow." This position is simple: With legs comfortably straight or slightly bent, drop gently forward
from waist until you touch, or if this is difficult,
nearly touch your toes. Rise back up slowly.

10. Sit on the floor, stretch your legs out in front of
you, hands on knees, as you exhale. Back straight,
stretch your head down to your knees, hold for ten
seconds. Come slowly back up, as you inhale.

11. An essential rule to remember: Always reverse the
postures. The reverse posture is known as "The
Cobra." Stretch out on the floor, facedown. Stretch
the upper part of your body upward, as you inhale,
hands under your shoulders on the floor. Look
upward. Hold for ten seconds, come down slowly.
Exhale. Resume a relaxed position when you are done.

12. This little introduction to hatha yoga should be
concluded with a breathing technique known as
"khapalabati," or "rapid breath of fire." This breathing
technique works amazingly well for spirit connection.
It involves a rapid panting-type breath, in combination
with a deep exhalation and inhalation. The inhaled
breath is held for five seconds, and slowly exhaled.

13. At this point, breathe normally. Keep your eyes
closed. Focus your attention on the point between
the eyebrows, called "the God center," or the
"third eye."

14. This yoga meditation should last approximately
fifteen minutes and be practiced once or twice a day.

There usually is spirit communication within the first week or two
of starting this technique.

Spirit Guides and Teachers

Do we have spirit guides and teachers, or is that a myth? It is true. Humans each have a band of spirit guides, teachers, angels, archangels, and departed loved ones. All are an integral part of spirit communication. You don't have to know who they are. They will work with you, whether you know who they are or not. It is their job. You might want to know that the job of teaching through spirit helps them. Spirits progress in God's kingdom through service.

Once Jack had a health problem that didn't seem to improve no matter what we tried. We decided to go to a spirit circle at a church in Ephrata, Pennsylvania, that did spirit healing. When it was Jack's turn to go up to the altar, I stayed in my seat and observed the healing. The lights were dim. Organ music was softly playing. When Jack stood in front of the minister, I saw a bright, emerald-green-colored configuration come completely over him. I saw the spirit figure of Paramahansa Yogananda standing next to him, touching his head and body. It lasted for about one minute. It was a very blessed experience, and Jack received a 100 percent healing.

While you don't have to know what your guides do in order to communicate with departed loved ones, it helps to have an explanation of the spirit band of helpers and their roles. This way, you can call upon the spirit guide best suited to address your particular problem or concern.

Your Doorkeeper

Also known as the "gatekeeper" or "life guide," your doorkeeper is in charge of your overall protection and well-being, from birth to death. The doorkeeper is different from a guardian angel, since the guardian angel has never been in a physical body and does not have as much of a hands-on, practical approach to your protection. The doorkeeper is not a relative, but is an entity that has been in a physical body. A doorkeeper has been particularly trained to function as one who guards the gateway to higher consciousness. Your guardian angel takes care of your more lofty pursuits, like deep meditation.

Your doorkeeper looks out for your best interests and stays close, both night and day, so that no harm can come to you. However, doorkeepers are forced by universal law to step back and away from you when a lesson of karma or destiny is about to happen to you.* This translates into "accidents" and other unpleasant soul lessons.

When you communicate with spirits, no one can get past the doorkeeper if it is not in your best interests. The only time your doorkeeper cannot do the job of protection is, as we said previously, when alcohol or drugs or Ouija boards are used. Prayer bolsters your doorkeeper's abilities and brings great power and strength.

Your doorkeeper and guardian angel are your primary protectors. They clearly have the most difficult, challenging jobs.

The doorkeeper and guardian angel oversee the other members in your angelic band of protection. They are your primary guides, always on the job, protecting you and lending the best guidance. They never have a day off, or go on vacation.

Other guides may come and go in your band, as your needs and development changes. However, the doorkeeper will never change. This powerful guide is always with you and is your constant companion. Also, your doorkeeper's personality is very much like yours.

Your Doctor Teacher or Guide

A primary force for people in the medical profession—such as a nurse, medical doctor, or chiropractor—this spirit teacher communicates information about healing to you. This teacher also transmits healing energy through you, to others, if you wish to do healing work.

Every time you lift someone's spirit, or help someone to feel better physically, the chances are good that your doctor teacher is

---

*Karma: the universal law of cause and effect. Karma is directly influenced by a change in attitude, which reduces the severity of the lessons we need to experience in order to evolve.

assisting. He or she was probably a medical practitioner or professional healer in his physical incarnation.

He helps to bolster your strength during times of difficult physical problems that are involved with healing. For instance, when you have to bandage a child's injured knee, or if you have to help someone with postsurgical needs or problems, he will assist you when you have to learn about healing methods to assist those around you. Doctor teachers can help in the most unlikely places and situations. For instance, the doctor teachers for mothers, masseurs, hypnotists, hairdressers, dentists, and physical therapists are very interactive, as are those for nursing home attendants and food servers. Healing can occur in the most unlikely places and situations. In addition, it can be done on physical, mental, and spiritual levels.

When doctor teachers do their work, there will always be some improvement in the person's well-being or health. That is, for those who are ready, or karmically allowed to receive it.

On occasion, when doctor teachers are doing their spiritual healing work, it is possible to smell the aromas of the substances they are using. For instance, when a doctor teacher uses herbs or plants, you may well smell eucalyptus, chamomile, or whatever else had been a part of his life's healing work.

Your Chemist or Pharmacist Guide

This guide works primarily with the body chemistry of people who do trance or mediumistic work. He or she is the primary helper for people who channel or do any kind of spirit communication work. For instance, your chemist or pharmacist guide will inspire you to drink a great deal of water before attempting spirit connection. This guide might also encourage you to eat a great deal of solid food after a session of spirit communication. The energy of the human body must stay harmonized and in perfect balance when involved with spirit contact. He specializes in helping to connect the physical and nonphysical worlds, on a person's chemical and hormonal level.

Your Primary Teacher or Professor

This guide specializes in helping people communicate at peak levels when they are in any kind of teaching capacity. Of course you can call upon your primary teacher or professor whenever the need for explaining, clarifying, or teaching about anything arises. This guide inspires, directs, and helps teachers to respond appropriately and accurately. He is also able to adjust the level of communication, according to the pupil's age and mental capacity.

Your Business Guide

As you may imagine, this guide may be one of the most challenged teachers of all. For many people, he or she has to help juggle books and stretch finances in ingenious, yet honest ways. Without this guide, most people would not be able to balance checkbooks, or deal with the monetary challenges of the modern world.

This teacher also helps people to know and understand how to reach the greatest financial success, in keeping with their personal karma.

Your Native American Guide

This guide specializes in teaching about nature, and natural healing methods. Your Native American guide will help you become more attuned to natural forces, occurrences, and events. This guide will help you to appreciate the beauty and majesty of thunderstorms, hurricanes, and forests. Your interest in flowers, grass, and trees will be increased with his influence. This guide will also act as a protector and guide, keeping you out of harm's way. For instance, he will keep you from being struck by lightning. He will also keep you from eating harmful foods or substances. He will shield you from toxic or radioactive situations. If you are lost, this guide will help get you back home. If your sense of direction is poor, call on your guide to show you the way.

When the occasion calls for it, Native American guides can manifest their energy, to allow themselves to be seen. This often happens after they have prevented an accident, or while they are helping to correct an illness.

One day, Jack and I flew in a small commuter plane in rough weather, from New York to Indiana, to attend a series of workshops for mediumship development. I don't usually mind flying, but this particular trip was so bumpy that even the flight attendant looked concerned.

We arrived safely and attended a spirit message circle the next day. The first spirit messenger who came through was for Jack. It was his one of his Native American spirit guides, "White Cloud."

White Cloud said, very clearly, "Jack, I don't see why Wife was so worried on the plane. Didn't you see me standing on the wing the whole time?"

Your Joy Guide

This guide should be everyone's favorite! This guide keeps people laughing and smiling. The joy guide will often be the shining star of séances or spirit circles, since the energy of the group has to be high. This guide will bring happiness and joy where it is very difficult to find, such as hospitals, sickrooms, or funeral homes. Joy always opens doors to greater happiness and uplifts the human spirit. Joy heals the body, mind, and consciousness, and even slows the aging process.

This is the guide to call upon when you need upliftment from depression, sadness, or despair. The joy may come in surprising ways, but it will come. When life seems overwhelming, your joy guide will help to make things more bearable. This guide will find a karmic way out of any gloomy situation. The motto of this guide is, "Smile! God loves you!" This guide often looks and sounds like a young girl.

Your Master Teacher

Now, don't become upset with the name of this teacher. Don't say that only Jesus, or Buddha, or Moses, or someone else is your "master teacher." This is simply a title that has come down through the ages. This guide is the one who heads up spiritual wisdom and philosophical teachings. Master teachers are especially involved with all causes related to helping underprivileged children, as well as abused people and animals. Your master teacher will be especially helpful during the greatest challenges and decisions, such as whether or not to commit to marriage, job changes, change of residence, or any other situation that is known as a "life marker."

Your master teacher also specializes in, and loves, creating synchronistic events. This teacher is behind your most life-changing and important events.

Your Muse or Inspiration Guide

This guide has the job of inspiring creative people, such as authors, musicians, poets, and artists. Have you ever received a brilliant flash of creative inspiration? That was probably the work of your inspiration guide. This guide is responsible for channeling to human beings great original music, great art, and all creative projects that inspire and uplift mankind. Does this guide also inspire works of a lesser caliber? Probably, if there is a need for mankind to receive it.

This guide helps humans to express the talents and gifts with which they are all blessed. This is the muse who will come to you when you hit "writer's block" or "artist's wall."

Playing beautiful music helps your inspiration guide bring out your greatest talents and abilities. Also, a quick trip into the shower when you need an answer works wonders. They specialize in flashes of inspiration . . . flashes that are so quick, that in many cases they are easy to miss. Keep a notebook or recorder handy for these moments.

If you need inspiration, call on this guide. He or she will more than try to inspire and lift your consciousness. After all, it's their job!

Mundane Guides

These guides do the most basic, but necessary tasks, such as running a home, cooking dinner, and fixing broken appliances. They specialize in helping us with domestic tasks. Domestic challenges will be decreased, and the job will be finished much more quickly, when your mundane guide offers assistance.

Ascended and Universal Master Teachers

These are the highest, most evolved teachers, and are of the caliber of Jesus, Buddha, Saint Germaine, and Mother Mary. In most cases, they have completed their earthly obligations and do not have to reincarnate on the earth. However, they are in service to mankind and will come when they are called. They will help out and offer assistance whenever they can.

Call on these master teachers when faced with a major life crisis, when you need spiritual and emotional support. They are ready to help, for example, when we are about to experience the death of a loved one or have already lost a loved one, or are in great travail.

Call for help from your teachers to assist you in contacting a departed loved one. Perhaps one or more of these teachers has been especially helpful to you and has made his presence known to you. You can call on him or upon the others. You do not need to know which one you are calling, this will be taken care of by your band of teachers and angels. The right spiritual assistance will be given.

A regular listener, Vicki had tried for years to conceive a baby. Both Vicki and her husband, Bob, had undergone every known fertility test and treatment, along with a few very bizarre and untried methods. Vicki began to call on her guides for help. Believing that she was receiving no help, she came to the conclusion that conception was not in her future and stopped treatment.

One night, while Vicki was in a deep state of meditation, she had an experience that she told us about on the air. Bob's deceased father, James, had been a physician. He came to Vicki when she was praying and asking for an answer. He said, "Vicki, this is Robert's father. You will conceive a baby when you are over water."

Vicki was so excited, she couldn't wait to find Bob and tell him.

"Bob, I can't believe it! I just had a fleeting glimpse of your father. He said we would conceive a baby when we are over water."

"Over water . . . hmmmm . . . a bridge? A bathtub?"

When she called into the show and told us what she had experienced, I said, "Vicki . . . I think you and your husband are going to be taking a very relaxing cruise this summer!"

Vicki and Bob conceived a beautiful baby boy on their cruise. They named him James, after Bob's father.

Out, out, brief candle! Life's but a walking shadow,
a poor player that struts and frets his hour upon the stage,
and then is heard no more. It is a tale told by an idiot,
full of sound and fury, signifying nothing.

—WILLIAM SHAKESPEARE, *MACBETH*

FOUR

Step Two:
Protect Yourself and Draw in the Right Vibration with Prayer and Affirmations

The Power of Prayer

Do you sometimes feel
That prayers are not heard?
Know that God and His angels
Receive every word.

Whether shouted or whispered
For a heart that is broken
Our Lord's ear
Hears every word that is spoken.

Angels always at the ready
At God's right hand
Waiting . . . then forward charging,
Ever at His command!

—Joyce Keller

Prayer opens doorways to new sources of inner spiritual strength. Soul healing and wisdom pours into our consciousness with steady, faithful, daily prayer and meditation. Angels and spirit guides are reached through prayer and meditation. Both prayer and meditation (see the following chapter) lift us into higher realms of consciousness and into states of clear reception in which we can achieve spirit contact. As such, prayer and meditation are primary keys to bridging the human and spirit worlds.

The easiest, best prayer before attempting to bridge the gap is, "I ask God (or the Universal Protector, or The Creator, etc.) and the highest teachers to direct this communication for the greatest good of all concerned."

Expect your first communication to be so subtle that it is easy to miss. For example, each day for a week, while Donna was praying, she heard the same words repeating over and over in her head. "Sock!" Sock!"

"What sock?" "Why?" She was perplexed, and did not understand the intuitive impression.

When Donna called into the show, she told us about the psychic message. I asked her, "Do you have a blue car?"

"No," she responded, "but my mother did." Donna's mother had died sometime previously.

"Donna, look in the car. I know it doesn't make sense, but your mother may have left you a surprise in a sock. Go look in her car."

When Donna called in to the next show, she said, "You'll never guess where I found the sock. It was in my mother's car. Actually, it was in her car trunk."

Here's the best part: the sock was filled with money and a bond!

Even if your first communication is as subtle as Donna's, rest assured that your ability to receive and understand spirit communication will improve with steady meditation and practice.

A Place of Your Own

In addition to the suggestions in Chapter 3 regarding the creation of inner and outer altars, you may want to take these steps toward refining a small, discreet outer altar in your home.

I recommend that you set up a small table in the corner of a quiet room. I say *corner*, because, as mentioned before, corners are the most psychically charged, most powerful part of any room. Cover your altar with a beautiful, white cloth. Add:

- Photos of departed loved ones and spirit teachers whom you would love to contact.

- At least one candle in a safe holder. The candle should be white, for the purest, most concentrated form of energy.

- A beautiful, clear bowl for water and possibly a small fountain if you have one.

- Religious artifacts that mean something to you and are considered by you to be sacred.

- A notebook and pen for impressions, feelings, and thoughts received in meditation.

- Sacred books, such as the Bible, the Torah, the Koran, and so on.

The strength of these items and their meaning to you will help loosen your hold on the physical, create a high, positive vibration, and help clear the way for more powerful contact.

Affirmations

In addition to prayer and meditation, affirmations are very helpful in reaching out to the spirit world. They are magical tools in that by voicing our desire, the results come more quickly. Spirits love rhymes and rhythms.

My spirit teachers have given me the following affirmations. Experiment with them. One will be especially right for you.

An affirmation should be said three times after an opening prayer that has special meaning to you, such as "The Lord's Prayer."

For Protection
Guardian spirit
Protect me with your might
Whether waking or sleeping
Both day and night.

To Communicate with a Loved One
Spirit guide of love
Spirit guide of light
Connect me with my loved one
No later than tonight!

For Clairvoyant Spirit Contact
Spirit contact, at my fingertips
I feel your touch on my eyes and lips
Come very close, let me see
Your brilliance in God's majesty!

For Clairaudient Spirit Contact
Guide so light
I know you are near
Please open my ears
Your voice let me hear!

To Keep Unwelcome Spirits Away
Guides of protection
Guides who clear
Remove all spirits
Who don't belong here!

To Soar to Spirit Worlds
Guide of connection
Help me get out the door
As I connect with spirit
Let my spirit soar!

To Communicate After a Loss
Guide of separation
Who helps with grief
Help me communicate
For healing and relief.

To Eliminate Fear of Spirit Contact
Guardian of light
Let me know you are near
Get rid of all fright
Please take away all fear.

Invite your spirit teachers and departed loved ones to teach you, guide you, and show you what you need to learn to succeed at spirit communication. They know what is in your heart and mind, but it empowers them when it is expressed. Don't hesitate to ask questions. Your spirit teachers will guide and direct the outcome of your communication for the greatest good of all concerned.

When Doug was told that his young daughter, Brittany, was diagnosed with advanced leukemia, his life went into a tailspin. His prayers for her increased to the point where they became all-consuming.

When the distraught father called in to the show, he said, "Joyce, the prognosis for Brittany is still not good."

The message I heard for him was from his mother. "Douglas, I am being told by your mother to tell you that Brittany will have a long, happy life. Tell your wife that you should both dry your tears."

I couldn't believe that I was really saying this. Suppose I was mistaken? I had to say it, though. The impression was so strong that I really had no choice. The words just came out.

Doug was silent for a moment, and then said, "But Brittany has only been given a year to live."

"Well, Doug, your mother is telling you to continue to pray, ask for a healing, and to expect a miracle."

Twelve years have passed now since I received that call. Brittany is doing well and there is no hint that she was ill. God and his spirit helpers, in the form of Doug's mother, delivered an unbelievable but accurate message of hope and healing.

As time goes on, your own prayer may evolve, of particular meaning and help to you. Remember, the most effective prayer is one in which we ask for guidance and enlightenment, along with the opening of the doors of spirit contact.

Prayer Beads

Prayer beads, used for prayer and meditation, are common all over the world and used by people of many cultures. Roman Catholics use rosary beads to pray the Rosary; Hindus use japa mala beads to chant; Tibetan Buddhists wear beads on their wrists; ancient Celts made knotted leather strands for prayer. Sacred beads have always been used to slow the mind and take the supplicant to a higher level of consciousness. There is no power in the beads themselves. It is the repetition of the prayer that raises our vibrations, and helps us to reclaim our relationship and connection with the world of spirit. The use of prayer beads helps us to create a path that goes directly to the spirit world. As the prayers are repeated, the everyday world melts away.

Making your own prayer beads, including the act of stringing and knotting, is itself an effective tool for spirit contact. As each bead is added, it holds and contains the prayer intention of the person who creates it. You can purchase a prayer bead kit from a religious store or craft store.

Lapis lazuli and quartz crystal work particularly well. Lapis lazuli, which was highly recommended by Edgar Cayce, and quartz, both vibrate at the highest frequency. On the other hand Austrian crystal, while it may be beautiful, is lead crystal and vibrates at an extremely low level because of its dense frequency and vibration. Therefore, it should be avoided.

Chants

"Aum mane padme aum," which means "The jewel is in the heart of the lotus," is a powerful Hindu chant. Also, the repetition of "Aum namo, bhagavatae, vashu de vaya," or just the repetition of "aum" (pronounced "ohm"), does wonders in raising the frequency and ability to connect to the other side. Many religions find chanting to be one of the basic techniques for connecting to God and the spirit world. In addition to connecting us with our creator, these mantras connect us to our spirit loved ones.

It is not superstitious to believe that God answers prayers that request spirit contact. Do you remember back in 1985 when Hurricane Gloria was violently working its way up the Atlantic Coast? My daughter Elaine was getting married that October on Long Island, where we lived. Hurricane Gloria had caused power to be out for thousands of us, and Long Island was seriously flooded.

Elaine was getting married the Sunday during the week the hurricane was due to hit. The day before the hurricane struck Long Island, Elaine called from her home in New York City, and in a panic, pleaded, "Please, protect my wedding dress and veil." Of course, even though I had no idea how it was possible, I reassured her that everything would be fine, wonderful, and perfect. I started to perspire, as only the worried mother-of-the-bride can perspire. I decided that the only thing I could do was say a prayer and go to sleep. While the wind and rain were howling outside and Jack was boarding up windows, I took Elaine's bridal finery and laid it out on a couch. I said a prayer for her wedding, then stretched out on top of her bridal outfit to keep it protected and dry.

I fell into a deep sleep. My spirit teacher, Babaji, came to me in a dream, and said, "Don't worry, Joyce. I will put up my hand, like this (he held a flat palm in front of my face), and make the storm stop right at the Great South Bay, in West Islip (our hometown). I promise that you will have proof of this after the wedding." He continued, "Elaine will have perfect weather, and the most beautiful, blessed wedding."

Amazingly, the wind, which had been increasing all afternoon and evening, began to slacken. The storm grew less severe and the rain stopped well before dawn. It was, indeed, as if a mighty power had put up a protecting hand to block the storm from coming onto the south shore of Long Island. Most amazing of all, though, was what occurred the next day. When Jack and I were watching WABC-TV news, the newscaster held up a map of the Long Island. The weatherman pointed to the exact spot on the map that Babaji had shown me, and said, "Hurricane Gloria stopped abruptly, right here in the Great South Bay, just before it entered West Islip."

We all were very relieved, but the wind had caused widespread power outages throughout Long Island. The day of the wedding approached and our power was still out. Sunday morning, the day of the wedding, Elaine and her bridal party assembled at our house, resigned to getting dressed and made up without electric lights. Again I implored Babaji, "Please get our power turned on, if it wouldn't be too much trouble." In my inner consciousness, I heard Babaji say that it would be done.

Our power came back on about two hours before the wedding, and as Babaji had promised, everything was perfect, including the weather.

The lesson is: Our prayers are heard and are answered.

Prayers are definitely heard, honored, and answered within the parameters of God's kingdom. If you ask honestly for spirit communication, and are mentally and psychologically healthy, your prayers will eventually be realized.

Prayer gives us access and acts as a bridge to the world of spirit. It is a powerful spiritual tool that will safely link us to higher worlds.

FIVE

Step Three: Strengthen Your Connection Through Meditation

Do you have the patience to wait until the mud
settles and the water is clear? Can you remain
unmoving until the right action arises by itself?
This is the secret of meditation.

—Lao-tzu, Chinese philosopher
and founder of Taoism

Meditation, which is also know in metaphysical teachings as "going into the silence" or as the "gateway to heaven," is an important step in spirit communication.

Meditation is the stilling of the conscious mind. By attempting to erase all outside thought, the mind becomes receptive to an inflowing or downpouring of cosmic energy. Meditation strengthens the connection between the seen and unseen worlds that are believed to be connected by an invisible "silver thread" that breaks at the moment of death. The silver thread is called the "sutratma" in Vedantic teaching, and the "life thread" in Western philosophies.

Meditation clears away the heavy, dense vibrations that surround each person on the earth, and makes spirit communication much easier. It encapsulates human beings in a shell of protection, especially when the person precedes meditation with prayer. Meditation grounds people who may be a little flighty and not quite centered. It safely links us to the highest spiritual power in the universe.

Meditation also increases creativity and intelligence, as it links us with the greatest power, or with God.

One way of understanding the process of meditation is to think of a lake that is murky from a great deal of activity. As the action on the lake stops and things grow quiet, the lake becomes increasingly clear. Finally, it is perfectly clear and is easy to see through it to the bottom. When this moment occurs in meditation, it brings a great connection to the spirit world. In addition, controlled meditation may well bring the enlightenment of the soul, also known as "universal consciousness," or knowing God.

Daily meditation, for fifteen to twenty minutes, twice a day, causes immense positive change in our consciousness. At first we might not notice anything at all, or we might simply notice that we are less stressed and irritated by our environment. Perhaps we make that desired spirit contact soon after beginning meditation. Maybe there's just a greater knowingness or understanding of the spirit world. Eventually, though, after steady, disciplined meditation sessions, you will begin to reap the reward.

Hopefully, it won't be long before you experience a breakthrough. At first it might be a flash of light, or you may see a sunburst of color while your eyes are closed. Your breakthrough to the spirit world may be heralded by hearing the roll of distant thunder or the sound of faraway bells.

One of the early and most pleasant experiences you may have

during meditation is what I call a crown of light. During a very deep state of meditation, you might experience what feels like a light hat placed on your head, along with a visual show of beautiful white flashes and streaks. You are likely to experience this on a deep, internal level, not on a physical level. This experience is coupled with a feeling of jubilation and well-being.

How to Meditate

Meditation is most effective when done at the same time and place each day. Try meditating in keeping with the earth's cycle, which means at dawn and dusk, to harmonize with the earth and its energy. Each session should last fifteen to twenty minutes.

It is best to sit in a straight chair, where you are comfortable, but no so comfortable that you fall asleep. It is not wise to lie in bed or on a couch or easy chair, since it is too easy to drift out of meditation into sleepyland. The yogis have for centuries suggested that we meditate in the "lotus position," which is as follows: Sit on a mat or bare floor with a straight spine, closed eyes. Thumb and forefinger touch in a "mudra" position, to contain the energy. In this position the hands rest on the knees. The legs are either lightly crossed, or tightly in a bound lotus position (see illustration on the following page). Crossing the legs in this lotus position does not cut off energy channels, but rather strengthens them.

Some people find it useful to have music playing during meditation. They feel that it helps them to focus. I personally don't like to listen to music at this time, as I find it anchors my energy too much in the physical realm and keeps me from soaring. I prefer complete silence once I begin. It is much easier then, to hear the beautiful, sweet messages from our departed loved ones.

In meditation, the goal is to remain calm and detached. You're watching, listening, and patiently waiting, all the while shutting out the things that are physical. The psychic, or nonphysical, world will eventually open to you. While meditating you will be directing the entire force of your being toward your high spiritual self and higher worlds of consciousness.

When meditating, use a place where there are no physical distractions. Your body temperature should be comfortable. Go to the bathroom first, if necessary. Ideally, you should shower or bathe first, brush your teeth, and blow your nose.

The room in which you will be meditating should not have any hot spots, such as bare, uncovered bulbs, which can be harsh and disturbing.

Location of the chakras in the lotus position: Ascending from the base of the spine to the top of the head.

You strengthen your meditation experience by working on opening the psychic centers of your being, called chakras. The chakras are seven nonphysical centers, or invisible "wheels" that run from the base of the spine to the top of the head. The purpose of understanding these chakras and working with them in meditation is to bring the energy, which is known in Sanskrit as "kundalini," up from the base of the spine, and get it to rise and energize each chakra as it goes up the spine.

Chakras

The best way that chakras can be energized and balanced is by doing the following:

Inhale through the nose for the count of five, exhale through the nose for the count of five. Eyes are closed, spine is straight, as you mentally connect with each chakra.

You can use the crystals that correspond with each chakra, and by holding the crystal in your hand during meditation, help energize and charge that particular chakra or center:

1. **Base of the spine, or root chakra:** This chakra corresponds with our most primal, base energies and expression, running the gamut from violence to blissful sex. Corresponding crystal is meteorite.
2. **Second chakra:** This chakra corresponds with reproduction; it is slightly above the pubic bone and is where embryos begin growing. Corresponding crystal is peridot, or olivine.
3. **Third chakra:** This chakra corresponds with the navel, or the solar plexus. This chakra, located right above the navel, is the center of the human body and the primary life-force center. Corresponding crystal is citrine.
4. **Fourth chakra:** This chakra corresponds with the heart and is exactly where the heart is. It corresponds with love and all human feeling and emotion. Corresponding crystal is rose quartz.

5. **Fifth chakra:** This chakra corresponds with the throat and represents speech and communication. The corresponding crystal is amazonite.

6. **Sixth chakra:** This chakra corresponds with the third eye, or the spot between and slightly above the eyebrows. The third eye is the window, or the doorway, to the spiritual world and controls ESP. It is the best passageway the mind or soul has for spirit contact. This invisible eye in the center of the forehead is known as "the eye of God," because when that chakra or psychic center is energized, it gives the ability to "see" the invisible spirit world. Meditation centering on the third eye helps us to ascend to celestial regions for the highest communication. The corresponding crystal is lapis lazuli.

7. **Seventh chakra:** This is the crown chakra, found at the top of the head. It goes directly upward to God and the universe. The corresponding crystals are amethyst and moldavite.

The ultimate goal of meditation is the energizing or illumination of the top or crown chakra. When this occurs, spirit communication becomes very easy and amazing!

Kundalini

"Kundalini power," the psychic energy that lies dormant at the base of the spine, is a very dynamic vital power. When kundalini is released during meditation, it often manifests by creating a great feeling of heat in the spine, dizziness, a whirling sensation, and often a feeling of altered consciousness.

As spirit communication becomes closer, there is a feeling of great joy, love, and knowing that feels quite euphoric. Through daily meditation, the power of kundalini becomes easier to use, and more controllable. As this successful use of kundalini continues, our ability to communicate with spirits increases. In addition, you should come out of meditation feeling as if you had a great night's sleep, or a perfect vacation. Your creativity and intuition will also be increased. You will have greater control over your entire life and an even more positive outlook. Your attitude should be so positive and uplifting, that all people who come into your vibration can feel uplifted from being in your presence.

Steady, faithful meditation, twenty to thirty minutes a day, once or twice a day, should also reward you with increased stamina, and a better state of health and well-being. Most people find that they have little or no desire to overeat, smoke, or involve themselves in destructive activities, such as drug or alcohol abuse.

Meditation and Breath Control

An important part of meditation has to do with breath control, which is known in Sanskrit as "pranayama." The following "Five-Breath Technique" will quickly lead you into a state of deep relaxation, inner stillness, and attunement for spirit communication.

Begin by closing your eyes. Count to yourself while you breathe in through your nose, 1, 2, 3, 4, 5, and then hold that breath for five seconds, 1, 2, 3, 4, 5. Slowly exhale for five seconds, 1, 2, 3, 4, 5.

Do this procedure as many times as is necessary to attain a state of complete relaxation. You should feel that your conscious thoughts are being eliminated, and that you are as relaxed as a rag doll.

Keep your spine in a straight line, so that kundalini can rise up easily through your psychic centers. The primary requisite is a straight spine, with no bad, slumped posture. This allows for the free flow of psychic energy from the base of the spine to the top of the head. When we are slumped, the energy does not flow as easily or as freely. You should consider doing yoga postures before meditation to make sure that the energy is free flowing.

Using Meditation for Spirit Contact

Have a large glass of water close by, which you will pour out after meditation. As mentioned earlier, this is not for drinking, but rather for a clearing and accumulation of energy.

Many people find it helpful in addition to prayer to read a sacred book before meditation. You can also elevate your vibratory level by reading books of high vibration, such as the writings of Paramahansa Yogananda, including *Autobiography of a Yogi,* or the books that have been written about Edgar Cayce.

While reaching toward higher spirit worlds in meditation, keep in mind the thought, "Be still, and know that I am God." Picture in your mind a plain, blank wall. Try to see in your mind's eye the person you would most like to contact. It will help to empower and strengthen the link between you and higher worlds.

The Steps

1. Deep, slow, controlled breathing, or what is known in yogic teachings as pranayama.
2. Use prayer for guidance and protection.
3. Uplift your thoughts. Think of the departed loved ones whom you would most like to contact. Surround them with a warm, loving, pink light.
4. Keep your eyes closed.
5. Direct your energies toward the third-eye area of the forehead.
6. Gentle, soft music may or may not be playing.
7. Softly mention the names of the departed loved ones whom you would like to contact.
8. Call on the highest spirit teachers and God to assist you in your spirit communication.
9. Remember the old adage, "When the student is ready, the teacher appears," and ask the universe to assist you.
10. Always express gratitude to the unseen teachers and loved ones who are working with you. They need to hear, feel, and know that you are grateful. This is a love-gram for them!

Do not attempt to meditate if you have been using mind-altering drugs, hallucinogens, or alcohol. These substances can bring in unwelcome energies, since they are very capable of diminishing your auric shield of protection.

Bill was in meditation, at the beach, when he heard his departed father's voice. He clearly heard, softly, in his head, "Willy, please . . . please do not go into the water. Do not go surfing for three days!"

Bill was shocked. It was beautiful weather. Wait three days to go surfing?

He considered going into the surf anyway, but his father's warning stopped him in his tracks. He did not go surfing. He went home instead.

Soon Bill understood everything. He heard on the news that there had been a shark attack at the beach where he was staying, at the time of the day when he would have been in the surf. The photo of his dad he used during meditation suddenly took on extra meaning. His dad was watching over him still.

Ways That Spirits Communicate During Meditation

Clairaudience

The ability to hear spirits as if they were standing next to you whispering in your ear. It is an audible voice different from your own and can be quite shocking at first. Another aspect of clairaudience is when the words seems to come from inside your head. With practice you will soon learn to discern whether they are your thoughts or those of spirits.

Clairvoyance

The ability to see spirits as if they were right there in the room and you could reach out and touch them. Another aspect of seeing spirits is a flash of an image in what is termed "your mind's eye."

Spirits can manifest as small, distinct, perfectly clear images, as well as an image of only part of the physical body, such as just a head.

Clairsentience

The ability to sense the presence of spirits, while not quite seeing them clearly, often coupled with clairaudience, or hearing a voice different from your own. This is a common occurrence for many people who experience spirit communication. It is also possible to experience the pain or feelings of the person who has passed on. It can be a feeling of suffocation, drowning or any of the many causes of death. This can also be coupled with the emotions that accompanied that death experience, such as fear, sorrow, and hatred. When that passes, the feelings should be those of love, calmness, and joy at the ability to communicate. Remember that you are in control, and do not have to feel or experience anything that you do not wish to feel or experience. If you perceive a vibration that is negative, simply call out the name of God, or of a being who is holy to you.

Using Scent

Scent, like sound, can induce a higher meditative, connecting state. It is a doorway to the subconscious, which doesn't have to get by the internal doorkeeper that tells us, "Hey, this isn't right!" "This can't be happening." "There's no such things as spirits."

Scent reaches us on a subliminal level and often creates a response before we even know what is happening. My mother always smelled clean and wonderful, with the very distinctive, feminine smell of lavender. Many times before I awake in the morning, my nostrils are filled with this lovely fragrance and I know she has been visiting me from the world of spirit. Scent is her way of making contact, just as we can use scent as a bridge to the other side.

The following aromatherapy mixtures have proved successful in achieving communication. Obviously, you need to discover which appeal to and work best for you.

Aromatherapy for Connecting

Frankincense, when blended with neroli, myrhh, and sandal wood.

Lavender, when blended with bergamot, rosemary, marjoram, and geranium.

Neroli, when blended with rose, jasmine, and bergamot.

Eucalyptus, when blended with thyme, lavender, and bergamot.

Ylang-ylang, when blended with lemon.

Pine, used alone, or blended with lavender.

Orange, when blended with marjoram.

Patchouli, when blended with bergamot.

Rose, alone or blended with jasmine.

Rosemary, blended with lavender.

Sandalwood, blended with neroli.

Incense

It's a good idea to burn incense like patchouli or frankincense while you are meditating. These types of incense raise the vibrations in the room, helping to cleanse and purify the atmosphere. Patchouli and frankincense are the two that are primarily used by the Roman Catholic and Greek Orthodox church. They have proven to be reliable for the purpose of purification, while also acting as a barrier that keeps low or negative entities at a distance.

Emmie was in the habit of burning patchouli incense in the mornings when she prepared for work in Manhattan's financial district. She would drift off into a happy meditative state before leaving for the onslaught of the day. On this particular day, she heard a distinct voice that sounded like her brother's, imploring her to stay at home. As she hadn't taken off sick in nearly a year, she decided to take this advice. Well, you guessed it. The day was September 11, 2001.

Don't use fruity incense for spirit work. Apples, peaches, pears, apricot, banana, papaya, or any other fruit- or food-scented incense will divert the attention from the purpose of meditation, which is connection to the highest spirit world. We will probably start thinking of a delicious fruit salad, or the fact that we haven't yet eaten lunch, if the olfactory senses are stimulated by these delectable fruit flavors, rather than thinking of the purpose of meditation, which of course is to raise the consciousness. No time to be wishing for a strawberry shortcake! Patchouli or frankincense incense, or the like, can attune the finite with the infinite.

Removing Blocks to Communication

The biggest block to spirit communication is that we don't really believe that we can communicate with our departed loved ones. That lack of belief sets up a tremendous block to communication. Know that you don't need to pay anyone to do it for you. You can do it yourself. As soon as you seriously put these techniques into effect, and start practicing them, your belief in spirit communication should become real and enjoyable.

The second greatest block to spirit communication is fear. Remember the words of the master teacher, Jesus, who said, "Perfect love casteth out fear." As you tread along the path of attempting to contact your spirit world, you will experience happiness. Your fears will be replaced by healing of the spirit. You set the pace.

The three secrets of meditation are sincerity, enthusiasm, and unending perseverance.

Suggestions for Spirit Contact Through Meditation

1. Let your heart, mind, and spirit be filled with joy. The greater the feeling of joy, the higher and more powerful your connection with spirit. Tears and sadness are not a welcome part of spirit contact, since sadness always lowers vibrations.

2. Playing music beforehand can be helpful. I have gone to many spirit circles where we were asked to sing to help

raise the energy. A favorite song that seems to be very welcomed by spirits (even if it's out of key) is "You Are My Sunshine." Frequently, music can work wonders and acts like a great spirit magnet.

3. Indian sage, also known as "smudge," should be burned, and all areas of the room(s) that you will use for spirit contact should be smudged before spiritual use.

4. Always have glasses of water around the room. Pour out the water when you are finished. Do not drink it, since it may have become infused with negative energy.

5. No electric lightbulbs, unless they are red and muted. No open candle flames near curtains or other items that can catch on fire.

6. No shocking noises.

7. Do not let anyone touch you while you are in a state of spirit receptivity, as it can be shocking to the nervous system.

8. The key to spirit/meditation success is practice, practice, practice. Practice spirit receptivity the same time every day, if possible. Be patient. Eventually your patience will be rewarded. The spirit world has to learn to trust you, as you have to learn to trust them.

9. In meditation, acknowledge, accept, and trust the information that the spirit world is gracious enough to offer.

10. Acknowledge God's infinite grace and capacity to offer us a new world of communication and love. Remember that prayer is speaking to God, and that meditation is listening to God.

11. The best time to meditate for successful spirit contact is 2 A.M. to 3 A.M., when earth vibrations are the thinnest.

12. Meditate for thirty minutes.

13. Cleanse your mind before spirit contact/meditation. No unkind thoughts allowed.

14. Meditate facing east, for polarity with the earth, and in the same place each day, if possible.

15. Your hands should cross the solar plexus, the balancing point between the forces of the body, when meditating or seeking to contact spirit loves on the other side.

16. While seeking spirit communication, seek God's face and God's ways.

17. An excellent mantra for spirit contact during meditation is, "Be still and know that I am God," or chant "aum. . . . aum . . ."

18. In spirit contact/meditation, your mouth should be closed, with your tongue resting on the roof of the mouth. In this way a circle of energy is completed. According to Chinese medicine, there are fifty-seven invisible energy pathways of the body, which run completely around the body, from head to toe, and back up again. These pathways are called meridians. The circle of energy is unbroken if the tip of the tongue rests against the back of the front teeth. This circle of energy creates the greatest human energy pattern.

19. Eyes should be closed at first, then possibly partially open and focused on a place on the floor about six feet away.

20. Don't be judgmental about your thought process; take your attention from your thought process back to the sound of your breath.

21. The ancient Chinese practice of qigong is very effective as a method of spirit contact/meditation.

22. Combining the burning of beeswax candles and Japanese flute music can work wonders in achieving spirit contact in meditation. It shifts the consciousness.

Meditation energizes the endocrine system, which is the spiritual center of the body. Through meditation, the cells of the body can become attuned to the spiritual music of the universal realms of light, space, and time. As your spiritual attunement increases, the bond between the spirit world and the physical world grows.

It is very possible to meet a spirit guide or departed loved one during a first or early experience in meditation. The roaring sound heard in meditation, usually the right ear, is an early sign of spirit communication.

Philippe, who was in the habit of meditating in a semicommitted fashion (when he "remembered to," in his words), received a message one day that was so subtle it was almost missed: "Drink you juice," the voice said in broken English.

"What?" Philippe asked of me the next week when he called into the show. "What does this mean, Joyce, 'Drink you juice'?"

It took me a moment, then I got it. "Did you have an uncle that used to read to you? I'm getting the distinct impression of an older gentleman who is holding a children's book. Now he's showing me the cover. It has a picture of a swan."

The silence that greeted me on the other end made me sure I had missed the mark by a mile. I was calculating what other profession to go into when Philippe answered, his voice choked.

"That's my uncle Martine. He used to take care of me. He would read to me about swans, which he loved. We had an arrangement that when I finished my juice, I would go to sleep. Of course I never drank it, and he would keep repeating, over and over in his thick accent, 'Drink you juice.'"

I have heard from Philippe, who is meditating and speaking to Uncle Martine regularly now.

You must make a commitment to yourself to meditate. The difference between reading about meditation and actually meditating is like the difference between reading a recipe for apple pie and eating it. Remember that the benefits of meditation are cumulative and gradual. It becomes easier to make spirit contact with each attempt.

Life never presents us with anything
which may not be looked upon as a
fresh starting point.

—ANDRÉ GIDE, *THE COUNTERFEITERS*

SIX

Step Four: Harness Your Subconscious with the Power of Dreams

God's finger touched him, and he slept.

—ALFRED, LORD TENNYSON

Dreams are usually subconscious memories or thoughts and feelings from childhood, extraneous moments in our lifetime, or passing thoughts and feelings. Past-life memories often surface in dreams as well, and may sometime manifest in nightmares as we relive actual unpleasant experiences or the death experience itself. However, the dreams that are not messages from our subconscious or past-life memories are often direct spirit communication.

Spirit loved ones, friends, guides, and teachers communicate messages and use our sleep time for communication of a variety of training experiences. Who among us hasn't dreamed of being in a schoolroom or of being trained for something that he can't remember? There are astral (nonphysical) schools that we attend in the sleep state as a way of accelerating our soul's growth. Contact is often easier while we're asleep because we're protected and can go to distant dimensions and planes.

Though dreams are the easiest way of making spirit contact, we don't always remember in our waking hours the experience we've had with our loved ones—we have a feeling rather than the actual memory.

Let's change that.

Keep a Daily Dream Diary

Spirit messages and greetings become clearer when they are recorded. Keep a notebook by your bed so you can jot things down and create a record. This will help you analyze your dreams.

1. Before you go to sleep, ask for the spirit communication to be as clear as possible.
2. If the messages are cloaked in universal symbology as they usually are, hang in there. For example, seeing a baby in meditation or a dream state usually means "a new beginning." There are many dream books that explain symbology, but one that I recommend is Zolar's dream book (see the Resources section).
3. Record as much as you can, as thoroughly as you can, and as quickly as you can, before you forget the details.

Do this, and I promise you, your dreams will become clearer, more easily interpreted, and more easily understood.

Most spirit loved ones resign themselves pretty quickly to life on the other side. Things that were considered to be important while on the earth are usually insignificant after their death or "transition." In some cases, though, there are issues that cause the spirit to be troubled and to stay too close to the earth's vibrations. These spirits occasionally do not go fully into the light until the issues are resolved, and so might come to you in the dream state, when your defenses are down and you might be easily reached. If the communication is received in a dream, the message might very well be along the lines of an unresolved issue that arose after the demise of a person. It might cause a bit of distress or restlessness to the spirit, until it is resolved.

Do Loved Ones Really
Appear in Dreams?

A month after my dad passed away, he came to me while I was sleeping. He said, "It's not your fault, but two of my requests that I wished to have followed after my death were not honored. One, I had always said that I wanted to be buried with my wedding ring left on my hand. I'm sorry to say that it was removed and now it's gone." He looked very sad as he continued. "Also, I had always promised Scotty (my son) that he could have my wooden clothing valet. I know he didn't receive it. Please tell Scotty that I'm very sorry for this. Also, tell everyone that things are fine here. Love to everyone."

While I am not able to say if my father's ring had been removed, it was true that my son didn't receive the valet and it went to a different family member. Nonetheless, my father looked much more peaceful having spoken about two issues that were very important to him. Having voiced his true intent he smiled at me, gave me a wave, and disappeared.

Quite a few months passed before I heard from him again, at which time he was much more at peace. He came during another dream with an amazing message. Before his death, my dad had been in a coma for a week. At that time he seemed to be straddling an in-between state, where he was neither in the physical nor the nonphysical state. My husband, Jack, and I spent quite a bit of time while Dad was in this coma, whispering in his ear, "Dad, either come back to us, or go into the light. Look for the light . . . do you see it? Don't be afraid . . . come back to us, or go into the light." We also quietly chanted the sound of "om," knowing that om, or aum, is known as the "sound of God," the most basic, highest vibration in the universe.

When Dad came to me the second time after his passing, he said, "I want to thank you and Jack. I would never have believed it, because I never believed in such things, but hearing the sound of 'om' was very helpful. That, along with you telling me to 'go into the light' made it easy for me. Most folks are given three opportunities to go into the light. It's best to get it on the first try, like I did. A big thank-you to both of you!" He smiled, gave another wave, and disappeared again—for a while.

The following is another visit from the spirit world that involves my late chiropractor, Dr. Gordon Davidson. Dr. Davidson was a wonderful healer and good friend. One night, he came to me in a dream. An avid golfer, he was dressed in a golf cap, golf shirt, and plaid pants. He looked at me and said, "I came to say good-bye. I don't belong here anymore." He blew me a kiss, got into a little golf cart, and drove into a tunnel. The next day I heard that he had died during the night . . . right after midnight, when I had dreamed about him.

I also had a joyful spirit reunion with my mother in a dream. In life my mother had been physically handicapped and unable to walk unaided since the age of sixteen. She used crutches to walk and was also dependent upon a heavy leg brace. Three days after her passing she woke me up, and joyfully announced, "Joy, look at this. Look what I can do!" She threw her crutches and brace away, ran over a hill, ran back, and then disappeared over that same hill! Eventually she came back and said to me, "Please don't be sad for me. This is so much better. I'm free now, and I feel terrific!"

As I said, spirit-contact dreams are almost always therapeutic and uplifting.

Recalling Dreams

Edgar Cayce, known as "the Sleeping Prophet," recommends the
following technique for the best use of dreams we receive from the
spirit world:

- Keep a notebook beside your bed. Record your dreams
  as soon after waking as possible.

- Suggest to yourself every night as you fall asleep, "I will
  make the best spirit contact I can and I will be able to
  remember all that I experience."

- If you wake during the night, write down your main
  thoughts and entire dreams will often come back in the
  morning.

- Train yourself to keenly observe your dreams for spirit
  contact. Give yourself the self-suggestion before going
  to sleep.

- Look for all aspects of spirit components in your dreams:
  the setting, the people, the action, the colors, the feelings,
  and the words communicated. Work on analyzing your
  dreams every day, otherwise the spirit world will be
  reluctant to interact with you in your dream state, as they
  need to gain confidence in you.

In the excellent *Harvesting Dreamland: A Course in Self-Discovery
and Self-Mastery,* the author Craig Webb recommends several
steps for improved dream recall.

The first step is to make a consistent effort to remember and to
record your dreams.

Before sleep, reread your previous dreams from your journal. This will allow you to connect with your dream memory.
It's also an opportunity to interpret your dreams and spot connections.

As you go to bed, clearly suggest to yourself to remember all of your dreams when you awaken either in the morning or during the night.

Anytime you awaken, keep your eyes closed, or shut them again, and remain as motionless as possible. If you moved since waking, return to your earlier body position. Gather as many images, feelings, or impressions as you can, then rise and immediately record them using a bedside journal or tape recorder, no matter how brief or vague they may at first seem. You'll be surprised at how much more you can remember as you write, speak, draw, paint, and so on.

In addition, be patient and persistent. Although most people start having success the first week or two, dream recall is a mental muscle that may require some time to get back into shape. If your recall is poor, trust that it will come in time. Trying too hard or being too serious can limit your progress.

Understanding Dreams

If dreams are illogical, five reasons are possible: 1. Only fragments of the dream have been recalled. 2. The dream is reflecting something illogical in the dreamer's life. 3. Mental blocks have erased your recall. 4. The dream is symbolic and needs to be interpreted according to the dreamer's understanding of symbols. For instance, dreaming of a baby usually means a new beginning. 5. The dream actually is spirit communication and not necessarily easy to grasp or understand.

If you are unable to understand a dream's message from the spirit world, suggest to yourself, before your next sleep state, that the dream repeat itself more clearly.

On Timmy's first day of kindergarten, he was excited and ready to start the new adventure called "school." However, it didn't happen. His mother, Marie, a regular caller to our show, received a hazy warning from her deceased mother.

Marie's mother, Rose, came to her in a dream, and said, "Marie, don't send Timmy to school."

Marie was puzzled. She called the show. "Joyce, tomorrow is the first day of school. What do you think?"

After tuning in to the situation for a moment, I said, "I believe the situation is related to an infection or illness. Why not ask your mother to clarify this for you before you go to bed tonight?"

Marie did this, and this time her mother repeated the warning more clearly. "Don't send Timmy to school tomorrow. It isn't safe."

It turned out that the school bus driver who would have picked up Timmy was diagnosed with a case of infectious hepatitis. Even though he only drove the bus one day, all of the children who rode on the bus that day had to receive gamma globulin shots, to protect them from the illness.

I believe there is an important message here. It is that we grow on both sides of the veil, when spirit loved ones are allowed to help us or work with us.

Nightmares, which bring with them an inability to move or cry out, often indicate the wrong diet or a lack of spiritual attunement. As mentioned before, nicotine, alcohol, and other abusive substances lower our vibration and make it easier for negativity to pass through us. Likewise, an unhealthy diet high in fat (and particularly red meat), refined sugars, and simple carbohydrates make us more "earthbound," in other words, easier for imbalance and illness to occur. Consuming lots of water, fresh juices, vegetables, and whole grains feeds our bodies and enriches the soul.

To end nightmarish dreams change your diet. Do what you can to erase any negative behavior from your life.

Dreams that are unchanged through the years mean that the messages from the spirit world remain the same, and indicate that the dreamer is resistant to change.

Dreams of ill health can be literal or symbolic warnings.

When a problem confronts you, ask in prayer for your spirit world to guide and offer you information through your dreams.

Be practical in your interpretations. Always look first for a lesson to be learned. Is there anything that you have refused to face, or something you've ignored?

Carefully observe recurring dreams, as well as dreams that seem connected. These dreams often indicate messages from your spirit world and illustrate progress or failure.

Tom, a teacher, was used to walking to school each day along one particular route. For ten years, he followed the same path. For a period of time now, his deceased brother, John, was coming to him in a dream.

"Tom," his brother said, "don't take the main road. Take the path through the woods."

Tom didn't know what to make of the message. He asked, "Joyce, do you think I'm supposed to change my path to school?"

I thought in this case the message was not literal. "Tom," I said, "ask for clarity in the message. Is there some other connection to a path that you should or shouldn't take?"

"Well," Tom replied, "I've been debating whether or not to go back to school for my master's degree. It's expensive, time consuming, and I still have to work."

Tom agreed to ask for clarification of his psychic message. Weeks passed, and he called the show to give me an update. He had asked for more information, and his brother stressed that he was to go for his master's degree.

"It will take me four years," Tom complained.

I told him, "You should listen to the suggestion. There is a good reason for you to do this, okay?"

He agreed, and added, "But I'm still going to take the short path to school." We both laughed about this. Today Tom is a much respected high school principal.

Dreams are the reaction of the inner self to daytime activity, along with the interaction of your spirit guides and teachers. Dreams usually show you the way out of any dilemma. So relate them to your current activities, because dreams may be retrospective, as well as prophetic.

Dreams are often from the spirit world, and come to guide and help, not to simply amuse. They direct our attention to errors of omission and commission, and offer encouragement for right endeavors. They also give us the opportunity to pray for others and to help others bear their burdens.

Dreams and Spirit Connection

Look for past-life experiences to be shown to you in your dreams. These are shown to you by your spirit teachers as learning experiences. These manifest themselves not only in color, but in the proper costume and setting of their period. They come to warn you against repeating the same old mistakes; to explain your relationship and reactions to certain people and places; to reduce your confusion; and to enable you to better understand life and your current situation.

Angela came to me with the problem of a recurring dream that she had trouble understanding and interpreting. Night after night, for a period of more than six months, Angela dreamt that she was drowning in dark, murky but shallow water. She also experienced head pain with this dream, and woke up each morning with a bad headache. When I asked her spirit teachers to explain the situation to us, they told me that the dream was caused by a death experience that occurred approximately one hundred years ago. Angela was still troubled by this drowning experience because at a certain level of her consciousness, she did not realize that the children she worried about leaving in that prior lifetime had also passed into the world of spirit. She was holding on to a death experience that required "soul-memory healing." When the situation was explained to her, and the healing occurred, the dreams and headaches ended.

Do not fear conversation with the so-called "dead" in dreams. If the communication is one-sided, it denotes telepathy. If both participate, it may be an actual encounter of spirit communication.

Dreams are primarily about self. Only a few dreams relate to family, friends, and world events.

Remember, persistence is necessary to understand the spirit world's messages. Try to understand spirit language and communication, along with dream symbology and the forms of language of the subconscious. (Look to the Resources section for more information on interpreting this.)

Give daily thanks to your spirit world, and to the creator, for all things. The use of daily prayer will also improve the quality and reception of your dreams.

Edgar Cayce offers this explanation: "During the dreaming state of sleep, we experience the different levels of spirit contact and consciousness." We receive input from the different dimensions of the spirit world. Through dreaming, we have special access to our spirit friends. Through dreaming, we have special access to our own inner spirit. There is not a question we can ask that cannot be answered from the depths of our inner consciousness when the proper attunement is made.

A dream may be of a physical, mental, or spiritual nature and may deal with all manner of psychic manifestation. These include telepathy, clairvoyance, prophetic visions, out-of-body travel, remembrance of past lives, and communication with beings in other dimensions, including deceased friends and relatives, spirit guides, angels, Christ, and even the voice of God. Dreams can also give invaluable information on the status of the body and causes of illness.

All subconscious minds are in contact with one another. Through the work of spirit on the subconscious, dreams may place us in attunement with those in the physical plane. We may be visited in dreams by spirit friends, teachers, and departed loved ones for many reasons. They may seek to give us assurance about their well-being in other planes of existence. They may come to influence us with their own desires or perspectives. There have been dream reports of deceased relatives appearing and giving instructions about where to find a will or a lost object.

When Claire called in to our show, she was distraught over the loss of her deceased mother's cameo pin and gold locket. It was her only tangible memory of her mother. She had searched endlessly, but could not find the jewelry anywhere.

When she asked me where I thought the jewelry might be, I responded, "Well, I see it wrapped in purple velvet. It's in a dark place, and I feel that you will find it within a week." I also suggested, "Claire, ask your mother to come to you in a dream or meditation. Ask her to show or tell you exactly where the jewelry is."

The following week, Claire called in again. "I found it! I found it! I found the purple velvet pouch that contained the pin and locket!"

I asked her how she went about finding it.

"I asked my mother to show me in a dream where the jewelry could be found."

"Was it inside a shoe?" I inquired.

Claire laughed and said, "Exactly. My mom showed me that it was in my closet, and had fallen out of one of my pockets into a shoe!"

The events we experience in the third dimension, the world of spirit, is a projection of what is being built at another higher level, in the future time of the current life. Therefore, when we tune into the higher levels, as we may in dreams, we become aware of what is being built and what may be projected into the physical future. Nothing of importance happens to us that is not foreshadowed in our dreams. This is not to say that all dreams are precognitive, or that the exact detail of everything we experience is given in dreams. However, the word *foreshadowed* suggests that we may glimpse and be warned of what we are building now which may manifest later. We call these dreams from the spirit world "precognitive" or "prophetic."

My cousin Mary was very ill with a terminal disease. One night, her deceased father, Joseph, came to me in a dream and said, "Joyce, I'm waiting for Phyllis to come over here."

In the dream, I replied, "No, Uncle Joe, you're wrong. It's Mary who is sick. Not Phyllis."

He looked sternly at me, and said, "I said Phyllis! Soon they will both be here."

I was shocked. My cousin Phyllis had just had stomach stapling and, for the first time in her life, looked and felt fabulous. She was so trim and happy that she wore shorts and a little tank top for the first time.

About two weeks after my dream, I heard the news that Phyllis had been in a bad car accident and passed away. Her sister died shortly after. Uncle Joe was right. Phyllis went first, and then her sister.

. . .

Just as the angels spoke to people in dreams in the times of the Bible, the spirit world still speaks to people today.

There is no dimension of human life, whether social, financial, emotional, or physical, mental, or spiritual, with which the dream may not on occasion deal. Dreams may encourage or reprimand, instruct or deceive, inspire or seduce, guide or confuse. The potential for an immense array of experience in consciousness is always there. What we actually receive from the spirit world depends upon our attitude, motivation, the measure of our attunement, and the extent to which we have made applicable what was received in earlier dreams and in waking experiences.

Many people want their dreams interpreted. Cayce gives the example of a young man who dreamt about his father-in-law who had recently taken his own life. In the dream a voice commented, "He is the most uncomfortable fellow in the world," and then the dreamer was shown his own baby crying for food. The image was to convey the dead man's hunger for guidance and spiritual sustenance. The next night, the dreamer heard the man's own voice, together with a wandering impression of restlessness. It said, "I need rest. I want to leave and be with my family down there." The dream contact had been authentic, showing the dreamer how much his prayers were needed for his father-in-law, who was still an earthbound spirit. He added that the reason the discarnate was turning toward people in earth life was because lessons are learned from that plane. The souls who had once been on the earth had to learn their final lessons on earth, where will is called into play, in a fashion different from existence on other planes.

Contact between the deceased and the living can be joyous. Sometimes it occurs because the spirit wants to show the living what death is like, to take away their fear and grief. Exploring the possible reality of such contact, one dreamer had her side pinched by a spirit friend so vividly that she screamed in fright. It was a warning about her health. Another had his toe pulled when he asked for it, and did not ask again. One dream took a man inside the brain of a relative dying of cancer, and showed him precisely what a relief death was when it finally came. A later dream also showed him how a soul feels when awakening to consciousness after death. Spirits are not only rewarded by recognition from the living, they can experience the joy of teaching the living. They can also, in relatively unusual cases, work directly with the living for the fulfillment of worthy causes.

Using Dreams for Spirit Connection

A few days of practicing dream recall should help ready you for successful dream connection.

1. Select the individual that you'd like to bring into your life.
2. Sit on the side of your bed and quiet both body and mind. Next, hold the image of the person clearly in mind for a few minutes, then lie down.
3. As you prepare for sleep, gently ask yourself to have and clearly remember a dream that reveals the answer as either an insight, an actual experience, or both.
4. As you drift off to sleep, keep your question in mind, trusting that the exercise will be successful. If other thoughts distract you, return to your focus.
5. The moment you awaken, whether in the morning or during the night, record any dreams or thoughts that you've had. At this point, do not judge content; simply record what you remember.
6. Reflect upon any dreams and thoughts that you recorded, and make whatever associations, interpretations, and waking-life connections that you can.

The answer may or may not be obvious, but trust that the process is working, regardless. Try to maintain a grateful appreciation for any guidance, impressions, or contact you receive, as it will promote further insight and future success.

Even if you don't remember any dreams or have little success understanding the dream experience you've had, rest assured that your dream experience, remembered or not, has had an effect. It may simply be simmering on unconscious levels and may come to you as a sudden message or contact during the day. The dream's meaning or experience may also only become clear at some later date.

A few years ago, I was intrigued and also bothered by a recurring dream about maggots. Around the time the dreams started, I had hired a public relations expert. I felt that my career could use the boost of some professional PR. I didn't fully understand the connection between the hiring of "Muriel" and the maggots, but I knew there was one.

Muriel and her firm were highly recommended to me by a number of high-profile friends. "Muriel is the best! You must hire her." Her skills were firmly trumpeted by a number of well-known TV biz contacts. So, completely ignoring the bad feelings from my dream world, I signed on with Muriel. I didn't understand then, as I do now, that my guides were offering me a warning in the dream state.

My friends were right about Muriel. She was beautiful, bright, dedicated to making me successful, and enthusiastic. For the first week, everything was terrific. Muriel immediately got me an appearance on NBC-TV.

Things seemed to be going along well. Then, while dreaming, I received a visual warning, this time from my mother. Muriel was dead, and she was completely covered with the maggots from the earlier dreams!

Hmmm. I couldn't understand it. Then, the second week, we hit a snag. Muriel's assistant told me that she had entered a hospital with severe side and stomach pains. She was diagnosed with an advanced illness and died within one month.

I felt terrible of course for her and her family. Most of all, I was reminded once again about the importance of listening to your dreams, which often contain messages from our loved ones in spirit.

Dreams are the doors to other worlds.

—Joyce Keller

SEVEN

Step Five: Establish a Special Environment by Creating a Spirit Space

Why fear death? It's the most

beautiful adventure in life!

—CHARLES FRAHMAN, THEATRICAL PRODUCER

Spirit Cabinets

The great, old-fashioned mediums who func-
tioned at the most mind-blowing spirit encounters often used a
cabinet, or dark room, for spirit communication. The cabinet
helped to contain and build spirit energy. In most cases, the energy
that formed the spirit manifestation was ectoplasm from the

medium's solar plexus or mouth. The use of an enclosed, dark space enabled sitters at the séance to see faces, or in some cases, full-body materialization. Unfortunately, the use of spirit cabinets has become somewhat of a lost art.

You can create your own cabinet for the collection and containment of spirit energy. The cabinet will allow you to be in an encapsulated, protected environment with no distractions or interference.

The spirit world is influenced and affected by physical conditions, such as the fact that the greatest spiritual energy can be contained in the corners of rooms, as well as where water is flowing, and at the base and summit of mountains. The spirit world quickly gets the message that a cabinet is specifically created for the purpose of spirit communication. They are delighted to have a safe, controlled atmosphere where people will not start screaming, be scared to death, or wet their pants. It's all very calm, cool, and professional. Everyone is happy!

All that is involved in the creation of a spirit cabinet is a completely dark, small, enclosed room, about six feet by six feet, and about six or seven feet high, and a comfortable chair that reclines fairly far back. If you don't have such a chair, use any that you like. Or, if space is limited, use pillows. Place a mirror on the wall opposite your chair, approximately at eye level. Repetitious, calming tapes, like the sound of the surf, may be played.

Obviously not all of us have room in our homes for a special room devoted to spirit communication, or room for both an altar and a spirit cabinet. An altar is more important and can be incorporated into your spirit cabinet. If you must choose between the two, use that to which you feel most drawn.

For those with space constraints, the semblance of the cabinet can be created by curtaining off a corner of a room. Sheets hung from the ceiling, room dividers, or even a curtained, canopied bed can be transformed into a "cabinet." At the very least, especially for those of us in small apartments, darkness can be achieved by blocking off windows, and can give the feeling of a small, dedicated space. I know of one person who uses a children's pop-up tent, which, when not in use, she keeps under her bed. Another uses her closet. But be wary of using candles in these spaces. We don't want any fires!

Prayers of protection should be used before embarking on the spiritual trip in your cabinet (see Chapter 4 on prayers). Go into your cabinet. What you're wearing doesn't really matter, but white is preferred, and it should be comfortable. It is respectful and uplifting to be clean. Remember the age-old adage, "Cleanliness is next to Godliness."

Before starting, spiritually cleanse the area by burning Indian sage or smudge incense. Patchouli incense will also work. Sit in your recliner. Listen to the sound of the ocean's waves. Let your eyes go softly out of focus, as you gaze into the mirror on the wall a few feet in front of you.

With regard to the length of time before you have a spiritual experience, it is completely up to you, God, and your doorkeeper. Stay positive. Don't let negativity or sadness creep in. Believe that you will experience results and in time you will.

Dark to semidarkness is best. You don't really need any accoutrement. It's all very easy, and the veil between worlds grows thinner with each passing day. Sit in the chair, relax, say a prayer of upliftment and protection, and let the spirit party begin. Be patient, as it may not happen immediately. Sooner or later your patience and diligence will be rewarded.

Try not to fall asleep. However if you do fall asleep, you probably need it!

Experiences with the Cabinet

The atmosphere in the cabinet is designed to create a feeling of privacy, intimacy, and safety. The understanding before entering the cabinet is that nothing can disturb you. It is totally relaxing, secure, and protected, because of the vibration you have brought into it. Many people who have had the spirit-cabinet experience have described incredible life-changing healing and joy.

A woman I know saw her departed mother very clearly when using the cabinet. Her mom was smiling the same sweet smile that she had always worn when alive. Other people have found the experience especially powerful, moving, and therapeutic. A listener named Joan, who had been unable to cry over the loss of her father, was in the cabinet for barely ten minutes when she "found tears flowing easily and with great healing." She heartily recommends it to anyone needing help with the grieving process.

Other people experience stress reduction. One of our friends, James, reports that regular visits to his own cabinet make him feel centered. In addition, he says it helps recharge his energies, and is a great first step toward generating spirit contact.

To sum up, the cabinet is a very effective centering tool that enables us to relax, focus our energies, and in many cases, make spirit contact in an insulated environment. It's a smooth, safe trip into and back from the spirit world.

Men have torn up the roads which led to Heaven,
And which all the world followed, now we have
to make our own ladders.

—JOSEPH LAUBERT, *PENSÉES*

EIGHT

Step Six: Draw on Your Senses with the Resonance of Sound

Seeing death as the end of life is like

seeing the horizon as the end of the ocean.

—DAVID SEARLES

Sound

Our Western culture is just now beginning to accept what most Eastern cultures have known for centuries: The sound of Tibetan bells and bowls reaches us at the soul level, and makes spirit contact easy. Tibetan bowls and bells are used primarily by Tibetan priests and monks in their meditative and spiritual practices. In actuality, the bowls and bells have been reliably counted upon for ages by numerous religious orders, not just

Tibetan. When bowls and bells are used, the atmosphere is immediately changed and charged with an energy of a higher frequency. The sound of bowls and bells touches the heart center and connects us to the spirit world in a beautiful, healing, therapeutic manner. As you attain a peaceful, quiet vibration, deep spiritual silence wells up from within your very being, clearing the way to communication.

When you think about it, what holy place doesn't use bells? Their purpose is not just to call the faithful to services. The sound is to raise and touch the highest consciousness.

Enthusiastic, ecstatic dancing to music that touches the soul is another key. Sufis have long used music and dance to bridge the spiritual gap. Music that taps into universal rhythms is extremely effective. Music helps us to awaken our higher senses and our intuition. It ignites and illuminates the soul and acts like a magnet for the highest spirits. Celtic music is another effective acoustical spirit bridge, as is much classical music.

Primal and exciting music, such as music with tribal or jungle beats, stirs and connects souls on both sides of the veil. Angelic music and serenades are also effective cosmic connectors. Irish soprano "Meav" is internationally acclaimed as having a voice that can help move you through many stages of consciousness.

Shamanic drumming, as done by Native Americans and most indigenous peoples of the earth, is a musical form of prayerful connection. Drumming is increasingly recognized as a powerful spiritual tool. In his book *The Way of the Shaman,* author Michael Harner explains that the beat of the drum is used to transport native peoples into shamanic states of consciousness, closely approximating the base resonant frequency of the earth, which can be measured scientifically.

The physiological effects of sound, particularly regarding altered states, have been well documented and have been shown to produce alpha, beta, and the psychic state of theta waves in the brain. For those who aren't familiar with these terms, there are four levels of consciousness. The awake state is "beta." As we become more relaxed and the brain waves slow down it becomes "alpha." Deeper, light to heavy hypnosis or receptive meditation, is "theta." The deepest, usually a state of deep sleep, is "delta."

The ability of sound to induce meditative connecting states was well known thousands of years ago to ancient Hindu and Buddhist cultures. These cultures have long used rhythmic chanting, singing bowls, finger chimes, and other methods to transcend ordinary consciousness. Drumming combines the vibrational tones of meditation and the 180 cycles-per-second beat, which approximates the frequency of the earth itself. These are all ways to tap into our higher psychic abilities, and to reach the highest levels of consciousness. Shamanic drumming opens a doorway to higher worlds. Shamanic, or Native American, drumming is a powerful, ancient tool to open doors of spirit communication.

Does It Have to Be Music?

Certainly, sound or music is intrinsic to spiritual evolvement such as the raising of consciousness. Second only to sight, our sense of hearing (inward or outward) is of utmost importance in communication. Throughout history, sound or music has been involved in religion and spiritual practices, as well as an emotional stimulus in worldly activities ranging from war (oh, how Hitler loved marching music!) to romance and love (waltzes and soft violin or piano pieces).

Etheric or heavenly music is the description given to beautiful sounds said to emanate from the higher realms. Humans have attempted to imitate this cosmic music, which some claim to have heard, in many ways. Some people think that beautiful harp music is the closest to the real thing. Others feel the sound of the voices of an accomplished church choral group is most like voices of angels. As mentioned before, pealing church bells are, to some, akin to spirituality.

Isn't it curious that our Western music is based on a repeating harmonic series of notes called the octave, which is actually composed of seven notes and that this number, seven, represents mysticism, spirituality, and religion? Even simple, pleasant songs like

"You Are My Sunshine," "In the Garden," and various basic hymns are sung in spiritual circles to raise the vibrations before spiritualist work.

But sounds don't have to be musical; the repetition of certain groups of words as in Hindu Sanskrit mantras, while counting the repetitions on japa mala beads, has a consciousness-altering effect. This is also true of Western prayers and affirmations. For example, repetition of the Roman Catholic prayer "Hail Mary" or the more universal "Lord's Prayer" seems to be empowering and able to raise consciousness. It can be the sound of a simple, single syllable word like *aum,* or *om,* that has a profound effect on our consciousness. This word is considered by many to be the primal sound of creation and is the sound referred to in the Bible as "In the beginning was the word, and the word was with God, and the word was God" (John 1:1).

Yet it does not even have to be a word that raises and shifts our consciousness. In meditation, with various changes of consciousness, we often hear sounds like distant thunder or the buzzing of bees. Even when fully conscious, we may be aware of a high-pitched ringing in our ears, which is called "the sound current."

Some of us find music to be an aid in meditation. I personally like Hindu ragas, especially those played on a sitar by Ravi Shankar. This music, to Westerners, is unfamiliar and nonintrusive. It tends to screen our other sounds that might be annoying or disruptive, while providing a relaxing, spiritual backdrop of musical sound.

Singing Bowls

Tibetan singing bowls are native to the Himalayas. They are recognized for their ability to mystically connect seen and unseen worlds. Their vibratory rate reaches the outer bands of the human range of hearing with a frequency so high that the sound can barely be heard by humans. The ringing sound seems to reach out and embrace divine realms.

Throughout history, singing bowls have been used as eating

bowls, sacrificial vessels, and as auditory tools for meditation. It has been documented that sound is energy, color, and form; sound can transform, heal, and most important of all, connect worlds.

My introduction to singing bowls was wonderful. I had the pleasure to observe the channeling by world-class psychic/medium Joan Riggi, and her associate, Joan Marie Powers. As Joan went into trance, Joan Marie invoked the help of the highest spirit teachers by calling out their names. She called on Jesus Christ, Sanat Kumara, Archangel Metatron, and a number of others. After that, Joan Marie held a singing Tibetan bowl on her lap and ran a short rod around the outside of the rim. Occasionally, she struck or tapped the bowl, which emitted an incredible, heartfelt, spine-tingling sound and vibration. The effect was amazing. As I felt the energy in the room change, the atmosphere seemed to become charged with an all-encompassing, loving feeling. I felt as if I were being bathed in a relaxing bath of warm light and love. The heavenly feeling increased, as Joan Marie used the singing bowl to assist in opening the door to higher worlds. After about ten minutes, she would stop, and there was a period of silence for about five minutes. At that time, Joan Riggi would begin the channeling session. It usually started with the spirit teacher introducing himself. Frequently, the voice that came through Joan said, "Good evening. This is Sanat Kumara, and I have come here for your understanding."

After that, the spirit teacher would speak individually to each person in the audience. Sometimes there were more than a hundred people. Each person would receive a very personal, uplifting, helpful message. I will always cherish my beautiful memories of the two Joans and the singing bowls.

Tibetan singing bowls come in a variety of pitches or sound frequencies. Many will not match the conventional Western scale of musical notes. Therefore, if you decide to purchase one, listen to as many as reasonably possible first. Select one that appeals to you on an inner level, and don't be concerned about getting the exact pitch that is right for you. In a sense, they are all proper for all individuals. Just select one that is to your liking.

To make sound with a bowl, you will need a beater, which can be just a short, thick, cylindrical rod or stick. However, since the tone produced is also dependent upon the nature of the beater used, it is probably wise to purchase a beater at the same time as your bowl. Some beaters have leather, rubber, or felt wrapping around one end. There are a variety of shapes, also. Select a bowl and beater combination that makes tones that are most appealing to you. Ask the salesperson to show you how to use them. If the salesperson or proprietor seems unfamiliar or unsure, find an establishment where the people seem to be knowledgeable in the use of Tibetan bowls.

Basically, sound is produced by striking the outside of the bowl or rubbing along the inner or outer edge of the bowl, circling either to right or to left. Place the bowl on a cushion or padding so there is not direct contact with a hard, resonating surface such as a wooden tabletop. This could throw off the clear tone of the bowl. Hold the beater lightly in your hand and tap the bowl on the edge, from the outside. This generally produces a long-lasting, strong tone. Try striking it in various places along the rim. Try striking on the curved outer surface and on the inner surface, also. There are no hard and fast rules here.

The other technique, and the reason they are called "singing" bowls, is to rub the inside rim of the bowl with a leather-covered beater. A short, thick, cylindrical wooden rod wrapped with plastic tape will do, also. As you rub the inside of the bowl, an increasing musical tone with many overtones is emitted. Continue to experiment with different ways of striking or rubbing the bowl until you find the techniques most pleasing to you. Also try holding the bowl in one hand as you strike or rub it and note how changing your grip on it has an effect on the tones coming forth.

Using Singing Bowls for Connection

The rubbing technique is the one to use with meditation. When you have achieved a smooth, steady sound, close your eyes and allow the sound to penetrate your mind.

Absorb the sound into your consciousness, shutting out all

other sensations. Try humming along with the tone. Practice humming until you can readily harmonize with the tone from the bowl. Chant the primal word *om,* or *aum.* Begin with your mouth open and intone the *A* (ah) sound for a second or two. Blend into the *U* (oh and ooh) sound and slowly close your mouth, ending with the *M* (mmm and nnn) sound. Repeat this, practicing until you can achieve a smooth, steady tone, in harmony with the singing bowl.

With or without humming or chanting, use the tone from the Tibetan bowl to relax your entire body as you go into a quiet, detached state, deeper and deeper within, reaching a sublime state of altered consciousness. Practice achieving this state often as preparation for quickly and easily reaching the state of consciousness needed for your connecting sessions.

Tuned to the primal sound of life,
The veils disappear.

—ANNEMA RAVEN

NINE

Step Seven:
Elevate Your Consciousness Through the Mystery of the Labyrinth

Death begins with life's first breath,

and life begins at the touch of death.

—JOHN OXENBAUM

Labyrinths are showing up in the most mainstream of places, including churches, synagogues, and temples, hospitals, parks, workplaces, schools, playgrounds, resorts, and retreats. They can be found in psychic and spiritual centers like the Edgar Cayce A.R.E. Center in New York City. Labyrinths are found are common to many cultures and have been respected and used for centuries. One of the earliest labyrinths is in the floor of the Chartres Cathedral in France. It was built around 1220, for the purpose of offering a spiritual journey for those who couldn't make a holy pilgrimage to Jerusalem.

Labyrinths have been embraced as a companion on the path of spiritual communication. They enable a deepening of self-knowledge. Walking a labyrinth creates a space in which to go into a deeper state of silence, clearing the way for greater psychic awareness. Labyrinths inspire confidence and calm even to those in the throes of life's transitions. Not surprisingly, they have also been shown to lower blood pressure.

Walking the labyrinth helps us to see our lives in the context of one who is on a spiritual path. Following its winding, yet defined path, one becomes immersed in the journey itself, the process of leaving behind, at least for that sacred time, the responsibilities and ties of the physical. As we walk closer to the center of the labyrinth, we experience greater silence, surrender, and connection with the divine.

Diagram of the classical Chartres Cathedral labyrinth design.

Labyrinths are used for meditation, centering, healing, regeneration of spirit, and connection to our spirit worlds. Don't confuse labyrinths with mazes. A maze can be frightening, entrapping, and might have a Minotaur lurking in its center! A maze can be higher than our heads, whereas labyrinths are usually painted, drawn, or imbedded into a dirt or tile floor. A labyrinth can be a small stone that can be held in your hand. As you trace the path of the labyrinth with your finger, it often leads to a change of consciousness. This is especially true with the large labyrinths, such as those that are so large that many people can walk on them at the same time.

I visited a church in Brazil that had such a tremendous labyrinth on its floor that I counted more than forty people on it at one time, with space to spare.

As the understanding of labyrinths grows, there is greater dissolution of skepticism. Labyrinths bring the mind to a place of quiet and bring the soul to a place of connection with God and spirit. This form of walking meditation often allows problematic past-life memories to be released, with a healing of the psyche. The energy of the labyrinth allows our spirit worlds to uplift, heal, and regenerate us . . . body, mind, and spirit.

Barbara, a regular listener, related a wonderful labyrinth experience. She had heard about labyrinths on my show and wanted to try one. While visiting her sister in Baltimore, she learned of one that had been built at a Franciscan monastery. It was empty, Barbara reported, for she arrived in the very early morning. There was a stillness in the garden where it was located, and there was only the sound of birds, and in the distance honking horns. As she walked the sounds lessoned. By the time she reached the center, the sounds had disappeared completely, and Barbara found herself in a wholly altered state. She hadn't done much preparation, and wasn't sure what she should do next. But in listening to the show, she had learned about turning within and just listening. This is what she did. She lost recollection of how long she was at the center; it may have been minutes or hours. But while she was there, she experienced a trip through a ravine, where she was led by her deceased father. During this trip, he explained that life was going to have some pitfalls for her, but in the end she would be stronger and happy. He assured her he would be right there beside her, to help when he was needed. Barbara said that such a feeling of peace and joy came over her that she didn't even notice that a group of chatting schoolgirls had entered the labyrinth. This had been the first contact she had with her much-missed father since his death, but after this she was sure it would not be her last.

A walk on the labyrinth is realistically and symbolically the act of taking what we have received back out into the world, along with a balancing of karma. Walking one is a deeply enriching experience. It is so simple, yet so effective. Walking a labyrinth infuses the spirit with the loving presence of the divine. It almost always gives an overwhelming feeling of the enrichment of the soul on many levels. Most people walking the labyrinth experience the strong feeling of the presence of their spirit loved ones. Many have heard their names gently called from the world of spirit, or have received strong, powerful impressions and important information.

As the meditative, connecting power of the labyrinth is increasingly recognized, many people have placed them in the most unlikely of places. I created a labyrinth mouse pad for myself. It's terrific, because using it with my fingertip or a pen increases creativity and inspiration.

Most people who understand it consider the labyrinth to be truly sacred. When you walk through it, let your feelings and desire for connection to God and his spirit helpers be expressed. Silently express your desires, and allow yourself to experience the feeling of divine connection.

If you decide to make your own labyrinth, it can be done easily by using masking or electrical tape on the floor indoors, or outdoors using rope, stones, or garden edging. For instructions on these and fingertip labyrinth patterns that can be printed on paper, see the Resources section.

Using the Labyrinth

There is no right or wrong way to walk a labyrinth. You may walk as quickly or as slowly as you wish. You may sing, chant, or dance. There are no rules. If your first labyrinth walks are uneventful, don't be hard on yourself. The labyrinth is different for everyone, and first attempts sometimes seem unsuccessful.

The main steps of the labyrinth are walking in, remaining in the center, and walking out. The first part usually involves the letting go of the mundane details and concerns of life. The center is a place of meditation and prayer. The walking-out part is symbolic of taking what you have received back out into the world, and incorporating it into your life.

Enter the labyrinth with an open mind and open heart. Be ready to receive guidance, love, and support from your spirit loved ones, as the bond between you grows stronger. The labyrinth will be a deeper, more transformational experience if at the moment of entrance, you clearly specify your desires and intentions.

Preparing for Your Walk Through a Labyrinth

- Begin by thinking of a question or issue that concerns you, and allow your spirit teachers to work with you.

- Think about what is important to you, such as clear contact with a departed loved one.

- Ask that your spirit contact be empowered and your consciousness raised.

- Express appreciation to your spirit teachers and loved ones for their guidance and support.

- Ask for guidance about how you can increase your spiritual growth.

The labyrinth teaches that we need to trust our sacred walk in life, and our higher consciousness. The formula is: home, center, higher power!

This walking meditation can bring great spiritual growth and insight. Tears can flow, along with healing and regeneration of the soul. Ponder problems, resolve conflicts, look for the meaning of life, ask for life direction, speak to God and his angels. Listen, and they will answer you. The spiral pattern of the labyrinth is one of the most basic, yet powerful, patterns in the universe. It appears over and over again, from a pinecone, to our amazing fingertips! It's powerfully encoded in the universe. As we tune into and connect with that spiral pattern, it can be truly transformational. It is a pattern of healing of the body, mind, and spirit. This is especially true for folks who are grieving or have suffered the loss of a loved one. Many people over the years have found this healing of the spirit to be very effective and real. It not only helps to heal the psyche, but allows greater connection to spirit loved ones. It may happen while you are walking through the labyrinth, or it may occur hours or days later. But it will happen.

In her article "Living the Labyrinth," Mary DeDanan explains that the pattern is meant to deceive expectations. "When you think you're close to the center, you turn—and suddenly you're far away. When you think you're stuck in the middle, one turn brings you into the core. Not unlike life."

The Prairiewoods Franciscan Spirituality Center, located in Hiawatha, Iowa, invites guests to walk a replica of the labyrinth located in the Chartres Cathedral in France. "A labyrinth, unlike a maze, has one concentric, circular path with no dead ends," the center offers as an explanation. "The path leads to the center and is a metaphor for the spiritual journey. The goal is connecting with the Spirit within us."

There is no right way to walk the labyrinth. Simply go at your own pace, when it feels right do so. Let go of outside interference. Calm the voices in your head that remind you of all the things you need to do that day. Rather, find that center of stillness within. Time has no purpose when walking the labyrinth. DeDanan explains, "When you walk the labyrinth with intent . . . breathing fully, letting go of your inner chatter, and then opening yourself . . . things happen."

Perhaps it's the focus on the task of walking and turning that enables you to let go of cares and worries; perhaps it's the repetition of a pattern that goes back eons. Perhaps it's just a sense that following the twists and turns will somehow, always, without fail lead you to the center. But walking the labyrinth creates a pattern within that mimics the one outside, and eases you into a meditative state where anything is possible.

Finger Labyrinths

A finger labyrinth is a labyrinth design that is traced by the finger rather than walked by the feet. Relax4life, a maker of finger labyrinth patterns and other intriguing items, explains that a "finger labyrinth functions in much the same way as a walking labyrinth, except that the user traces the path to the center of the design using a 'walking' finger rather than the feet."

Whether you use your fingers or your feet, labyrinths are truly a sacred path, an easy way of connecting to the Holy Spirit, as well as our departed loved ones.

You've got to walk
that lonesome valley.
Got to walk it by yourself.
No one else
can walk it with you.
You've got to
walk it by yourself.

—TRADITIONAL SONG

TEN

The Connection Technique: Using the Seven Steps

I finally believe in the continuum of life after what we
call death takes place. I believe there are two sides to the
phenomenon known as death, the side where we live,
and the other side where we shall continue to live.
Eternity does not start with death, we are in eternity now.
We merely change the form of the experience called life,
and that change, I am persuaded, is for the better.

—NORMAN VINCENT PEALE

Again, the Seven Steps for contacting your loved ones are:

1. Call on your angels and spirit teachers.
2. Protect yourself and draw in the right vibration with
   prayer and affirmations.
3. Strengthen your connection through meditation.
4. Harness your subconscious with the power of dreams.

5. Establish a special environment by creating a spirit space.

6. Draw on your senses with the resonance of sound.

7. Elevate your consciousness through the mystery of the labyrinth.

I hope you have focused on these concepts and begun to use those to which you feel drawn. Perhaps by now you have even:

- begun to work on your consciousness by letting go of doubt and fear;

- learned to call on your angels and spirit guides;

- incorporated meditation into your daily routine;

- begun to recognize the messages in your dreams;

- created a special, designated space that is holy and special to you;

- created a labyrinth, either indoors or outdoors, and have found some success in elevating and shifting consciousness;

- found music or sound that is particularly calming and significant.

Now let's move on to a guided meditation where you will initiate spirit contact on your own.

Using the Connection Technique

I am going to take you through a guided session. You can use the following session in any number of different ways, but my suggestion is that you keep this book alongside you for the first few times, reading this section through, then beginning, letting it seep into your consciousness. Practice with the book, then without, making the substitutions and changes that are meaningful to you and seem right to you along the way. If you wish, you may use a guided meditation tape (see the Resources section in the back of this book). Or, make a tape using your own voice, reading the words herein, then use the tape to guide you through your connection.

As We Begin

You will need a tape recorder, a clean, unused tape, a pad of paper, and a writing implement, as well as water to drink, and water to purify.

Have your crystals ready if you wish to use them, cleaned and purified.

Make sure there are no outside distractions or bare lightbulbs. Unplug your phone and put a Do Not Disturb sign outside your door. Close the windows and block off light.

Light your incense if you are using any, or apply your aromatherapy, and light your white candle.

Get your music ready, or your bells or bowls if you wish.

Connection is something we do all the time whether we realize it or not. Just speaking with each other or expressing ourselves is a form of connection. The connection we come to know and understand in a metaphysical way can be one of two types:

The primary type occurs as a conversation, where you're awake and you might be slightly altered in appearance and your voice might be different. You're channeling energy from a very high source. It might be from high guides, high teachers, from universal intelligence or universal consciousness, or from the God center.* It doesn't look like much is going on, but it's channeling. That's what many psychics or mediums do.

The second type is trance channeling, where you actually go

---

*God center: That point within us where we perceive our deepest, most quiet, and most highly concentrated energy as, through deep meditation, we withdraw into a state of complete silence.

into a trance. If you've seen this occur, the psychic might be rolling his head around, or other bizarre things might be happening. As connection occurs, the energy changes. It can be very subtle, with maybe just a closing of the eyes. After a few moments, a changeover in energy develops as the voice changes and an entity begins speaking. This usually includes an introduction of who he is, and what he hopes to accomplish.

Here, I can only tell you what I feel to be true and what I feel works. Since there is a lot of unidentifiable energy in the ethers,* some of it God-centered and some of it not, you will have to decide if you want to do this in God consciousness,† as, of course, I prefer to do. Then, before you attempt to begin connection, you should use prayer, visualization of white light—the drawing in of God's white light around you—and, if you know the names of your angels and high spirit teachers, call on them, use their names, and say them out loud. I don't wish this to be a religious session, but I know what works for me. I can only suggest that you do the same, calling upon, for example, Jesus, Moses, Muhammad, Buddha, Yogananda, or whomever is meaningful and dear to your heart. This is for both your protection, to disperse low-vibration or negative entities, and for the high spiritual energy that these masters impart.

Some Basic Rules

1. Same time, same place, and practice every day, if possible.
2. Begin with yoga breathing exercises to help center the body and consciousness.
3. Recite a prayer.
4. Call on spiritual masters or teachers who are meaningful to you.
5. Become very quiet and peaceful, allowing the energies

*Ethers: The atmosphere through wich fine vibrational energies are transmitted.
†God consciousness: An advanced state of awareness wherein we realize the connection of ourselves with all things throughout the universe in a state of oneness or integration with the creator.

to change over, enhancing an atmosphere that allows
the entities to come through and to adjust themselves
to you.

Usually when you begin connection, it's very hard to understand
what's being said. It sounds like some kind of mumbling gibberish
in the early stages—very quiet, very low. You should have a tape
recorder so that the entity can speak into the recorder. Then, if
you begin sleeping or if your consciousness changes and things
happen that you won't remember (I can't always remember in the
readings that I do), you'll have a recording of what was said. If you
are doing this in the presence of another or a group, assign one
person who will say, "Please speak up, we can't really understand
you." If you're speaking into a tape recorder, give yourself this
command before you start: "I would like this to be understandable. I would like it to be clear. I'd like my teachers to speak
through me clearly and audibly." Much of this can be controlled
by your own energies and desires.

Some of you may choose to use crystals. The amethyst is usually helpful if it has been cleaned or prepared properly (left in the
sunlight or however you choose to clean it). The amethyst is particularly helpful for working with higher energies, and so is moldavite—many people pull in high energy using this particular
crystal. Take your crystal of choice, hold it in your hand, speaking
to it kindly as you would to a dear friend, and ask that it focus and
concentrate incoming energy to make it clearer and stronger. It is
similar to the way that primitive radio sets used crystals to tune
into the radio signal.

You should be very comfortably dressed. I usually wear a sweat-
suit, something very comfortable. I don't worry about image, I just
focus on having nothing restrictive on my body, knowing that if
I wear a bracelet, jewelry, or earrings or anything like that, it's going
to affect my energy or throw me off.

No part of your body should be crossed, not ankles or legs,
unless it's because you're sitting in the yoga position known as the
lotus. In that case, it's centering you, keeping you from falling

over, and locking you into position. However, use the lotus only if you are already accustomed to sitting in it for long periods.

Let's Begin

This session is for connecting to the higher realms, to your loved ones that you may be missing, or to whom you want to check in on or speak to.

I want your conscious mind to let go of the doubts and apprehension and fear of ridicule. I want you to understand how you fit into connection, how your angels and teachers fit in, how the highest sources fit in, and how only the purest thoughts and principles have a place here, when you're connecting to a higher realm. Hear these words, allow them into your consciousness.

Start your music now.

At this time I'd ask you to get really comfortable. Do whatever you have to do. Some people choose to lie down, but you have to be careful you don't fall asleep. If you fall asleep it's all right—I have seen many great psychics channel in the sleeping position. Edgar Cayce did that; many people do. But it's better, until you get used to the energy changeover and to what you're doing—unless your guides and teachers tell you to do it that way—to be sitting in an almost reclining position. This should be a position where you can keep your spine fairly straight and you're comfortable and not going to fall out of your chair. Your guides won't let you fall anyway, but be sure that you don't have that worry.

Your spine should be straight because you have the seven chakras, the psychic centers starting at the base of the spine going to the top of the head. As the energy called kundalini—the coiled serpent power, or the unseen energy lying at the base of the spine—is released through meditation and through connection, the energy comes up the spine and crosses over each of the seven chakra centers until its released at the top of the head. With that release you have illumination, the opening of the God consciousness as it comes through the crown chakra at the top of the head and up to the oversoul—or out to the universe—pulling in and drawing down the energy back into the seven psychic centers going back down, anchoring you to the earth.

See this kind of looplike energy as you close your eyes. Feel the energy first coming from beneath your feet, coming up through your body, coming up through the base of the spine, coming up through the first chakra. See this white light coming and touching the base of the chakra, seeing it as a ball of white light touching the base of the spine, the first chakra.

Then, going to the second chakra, which is right above the pubic bone and is where life begins—if you know what the pregnancy experience is like you know how life begins growing here—feel that white light coming and touching that center.

Move the light up to the third chakra—the solar plexus, the seat of much of the energy that we use in our daily day-to-day life—see the white light as a ball of illuminated light touching this third chakra.

Moving up along the spine, feel the light touch the heart center—the fourth chakra and the seat of love. As that white light touches the heart, feel a releasing of love that permeates every part of your body and goes out into the universe as a loving warm vibration. See it, and release it.

Let this white light continue to ascend. It touches the throat chakra and illuminates this fifth chakra. As you continue to do this every day and go through the process, you understand that as the energy touches and charges the fifth throat chakra, you have a greater ability to express God's wisdom and God's light.

As that white light continues to rise, it again goes up, and goes slightly above the eyebrows to the center of the forehead—the sixth chakra, the eye of God. When the pineal gland, also called the third eye, is illuminated on a daily basis, you develop the ability to speak in psychic intuitive expression, and to have the God consciousness expressing through your third eye. Think of a string going down through the center of your head, across the center of the head, and touching the third-eye center—the pineal gland.

Then visualize the white light continuing up and illuminating the entire top of the head, the crown chakra, the universal cosmic consciousness, God consciousness, signifying oneness with the universe.

And then, continuing up, as it goes out, up into the high ethers—up into the seven planes, as far as you can imagine it going, up many levels of energy—it then turns back and starts descending. As it comes down and down and down, touches your head again, and once again touches your crown chakra, it comes back down and touches the sixth chakra, the fifth, fourth, third, second, first, down to the base chakra again. Let it go down through your legs and back down to the earth. Let it go down and anchor you—you are being anchored to the earth. Now, again coming back up through the feet, this white light goes through the body, to the first chakra, second, third, fourth, fifth, sixth, seventh, and goes back up—until you have anchored yourself.

At this time, after a prayer of protection and guidance, asking that the highest angels and teachers will be with you during your connection time. Choose a prayer for yourself, the Lord's Prayer, the Twenty-third Psalm, a prayer from Jewish, Muslim, Hindu, or other religion or whatever prayer you choose to say that is important to you, that you can relate to in the deepest parts of your heart and consciousness. Say that prayer to yourself at this time.

All right? Now we'll move on to a breathing exercise.

Relaxing every part of your body, breathe in deeply through the nose. Take the deepest possible breath and release, relax, and let it all go out as you breathe out.

Now breathing in for the count of five through the nose: 1, 2, 3, 4, 5—draw the energy to the third eye above the eyebrows.

Holding for 5: 1, 2, 3—seeing your head filled with white light—4, 5.

Exhale for 5, releasing fatigue and tension—1, 2, 3, 4, 5.

Once again, inhale for 5—breathing in God's white light, and seeing it as beautiful sunlight streaming in. Breathing in—1, 2, 3, 4, 5—seeing your head, and entire consciousness, your aura filled with this beautiful white light as you sit there radiating this light throughout your body—out through your fingertips; out through every part of your body. Holding—1, 2, 3, 4, 5 and then and exhaling as the light within you grows brighter—1, 2, 3, 4, 5.

Relax completely, going into a deeper state of relaxation.

There are many types of breath that can be done. The alternate breath is excellent also, because it blocks out any type of interference. We'll proceed to do the alternate breath now, as it works so well.

Take your right thumb, and close off your right nostril.

Next two fingers go onto the third eye between the eyebrows.

The last two fingers close off the left nostril.

Open both nostrils for a moment, exhale completely through your nose, then close off the nose.

Open the right nostril, and inhale for the count of 4—1, 2, 3, 4.

Close off the right nostril for 16—1, 2, 3, 4, 5, 6, 7, 8, 9, 10, 11, 12, 13, 14, 15, 16.

Then, exhale on the left for 8—1, 2, 3, 4, 5, 6, 7, 8.

And once more repeating, inhaling on the left for 4, close off, hold for 16.

Exhale on the right for 8.

Relax, drop your hand and arm, breathing deeply.

Realize that we are usually in a state of beta consciousness from moment to moment as we function throughout the day. As you go into a more relaxed state, you pass into alpha through the breathing exercises. Becoming more relaxed, perhaps going down to theta, realize that if you go more deeply you will be going down to delta, which is the sleep state, and which you do not wish to do at this time.

This is a good time to ask that your teachers or guides and angels come through and make themselves known to you or express through you. Ask for their names. If you know some of their names, invite them. If not, ask that the highest teachers and angels who would like to work with you be present. Ask for their guidance, their protection, and assistance in connecting with your loved one. Ask that they act as a spiritual shield to prevent intrusion by any low vibration or negative, uninvited entities or energies. Ask for their help in contacting those departed loved ones with whom you wish to speak. Ask that you be provided a doorkeeper guide for protection and help in making contact and maintaining order when there are a number of entities who wish to be heard.

At this point, open your heart and mind and consciousness to the higher energies. As you do this, proceed into a period of extreme quiet, which is known as "the silence." In this state you may hear voices and the expression of your own oversoul.[*]

Ask for the divine Holy Spirit to express through you and within you. Visualize white light around the recorder and microphones that you use. Think of the person that has been on your mind, perhaps thinking of a question that you've written down for this person before you started. Bring that question to mind, and know that if you don't get an answer in this session, the information will come through shortly thereafter.

Attune yourself to the higher life-force energy coming in, remembering to always have water in the room as not only something that will boost your power frequency, but also as a conductor of spirit energy and as a catch-basin of any negativity that may be in the room. This is not something you will drink.

Say aloud the name of the individual you wish to contact. Ask that this person be allowed to come through to you. Request that you see this person, clairvoyantly, or hear within, the sound of his or her voice greeting you. If successful, ask questions and express yourself, as you wish, to this individual: "Are you here in the name of the highest and most holy?" "Are you of God?" "What is your name?" "What do you know about me?" "Can you give me specific details about your life?"

If you cannot establish connection with the specific individual you seek, realize that the time may not be right, that the soul may

---

[*]The oversoul relates each and every incarnation and action of your self. It is the supreme, overarching expression of who you are and your highest purpose.

still be in a sleep state, or occupied at a different level of existence at the present time.

Ask if there is anyone who would like to communicate with you. Ask that the individuals identify themselves, and that they are to come only in the light of God, with truth and love. Sit quietly with your eyes closed and slightly raised. Listen.

If you feel any presence, ask another question. Ask if there is a message for you. Feel the energy that's around you as you ask the question. Understand that a feeling of heightened awareness and feelings of well-being accompany connection. Ask a question that's on your mind, and listen for an answer. Ask the person how he is doing, if she is happy. If you choose to have verbal expression, actually letting him speak through you, say any words that come to you at this time. Say whatever pops into your mind, or any series of words that comes into your consciousness. You might feel a sensation of heat or tingling, particularly throughout your spine. You might feel some shuddering, or you might feel nothing. You might have a feeling of floating or dizziness. All of these feelings are a rising of the energy called kundalini from the base of the spine and through the psychic centers. Visualize and feel an almost blinding white light around you as the energy manifests.

It is possible that you might try this many times before this energy manifests, or it could happen the first time you try. Continue to speak whatever's on your mind.

Some of you will want to try automatic writing. There should be paper and pen or pencil nearby so you can try to write down a message. If you prefer, speak into the tape recorder. There may be an important message for you from a loved one. Perhaps the message will be written down on your paper or will be heard on your tape later.

For automatic writing, hold your pen or pencil lightly on your pad of paper on a clipboard or desk. Go into your meditative channeling state while holding your pen, with your eyes closed. Ask that information be given through you directly onto the paper. Allow your hand to move freely if you feel any indication for it to do so. You might try moving your pen across the paper as if you were writing or scribbling on the paper until there is a definite influence to move your hand in a certain way. Use of a typewriter or computer keyboard is also feasible. Rest your hands on the keyboard and follow any urge to press a key. Try pressing keys randomly to get started.

Perhaps the best thing for you to do at this time is to just listen. Listen to the voice within, increasing the attunement each time you do this. What impressions are you receiving? What are you attempting to express at this time? Go deeper into the silence within. You are the temple. You are the sanctuary. Reach for the God within. Let your guides and teachers express through you. Use yourself as the vehicle. Increase your compassion and love for the universe. Request that your teachers bring in the highest God-conscious energy, and the person you are trying to reach. Receive on the highest energy level. Nothing else will be acceptable. Do you receive a name of an energy or an individual? What is the name you're receiving? Say the name out loud.

Feel the power come through you and feel the changeover of energy. What name or names are you receiving? Remember that many high angels do not have names; they're expressions of pure energy. Much of the work done on our inner planes deals with the expression of energy that is nameless. So if you're not getting a name, move away from that. You may be dealing with the expression of universal consciousness. Perhaps it's just an uplift in energy. Allow the beings of light to express that light through you, letting these beings of light offer expression, clarity, or direction, in whatever areas of your life they feel would be necessary. Let the high guides come to light your path, understanding that their only wish is for our higher good, for our own wisdom and for our discernment. See the light, feel the light; feel the protection. What are you feeling? What are you seeing? What impressions are you receiving? If it's just one word, speak that word at this time. If it's a sentence or paragraph or thought, allow that connection to occur.

Do you see a face? Do you have an impression . . . a feeling? What are you feeling, and what are you receiving? Is there a feeling of wisdom, comfort, or warmth? As you become relaxed and used to this energy as it manifests, more and more will be able to be expressed through you. Sometimes it can be the next day or at a time that you're not even aware of connection. You will find that you're speaking knowledge about a loved one that perhaps you've never expressed previously, or knew before. Perhaps loved ones are speaking through you at this time, or your own higher soul consciousness is expressing through you.

We communicate with spirit in many different ways. Allow it just to flow, in whatever way is right for you. Ask the question at this time: "Who is there?" "Who are you with?" "Is there anyone there, anyone who would like to speak with me at this time?" "I surround you with the light of God. Speak now, please." "If you are here and are of God, please speak." Understand that the highest consciousness is where you are using your own inner guidance, your own soul's expression, and the guides who come and work with us do that in conjunction with our own energy and in our own magnetic fields. They're not superimposing, they're not imposing, they're working with our energies. If you doubt that you're actually channeling, try not to doubt and just let it happen. The doubts are here to help you grow and to understand. They're a very normal part of development.

As you channel, you can see more light coming into your body. You become a lighter and lighter energy. It helps if you've been cautious about your diet, that you've tried to go off sugar and eliminated alcohol, red meat, and caffeine; followed a very healthy diet, being very respectful of your body, your mind, and your consciousness. Don't worry if you feel connection is only part of your imagination. It may seem or feel like that, but this is part of development.

As the energy is expressing itself, your telepathy is growing. Your clairvoyant ability is growing, your love for mankind is growing, and your ability to connect is increasing. Your ability to connect to others through the spoken word and through touch is growing. Channel the highest God consciousness; channel the highest energy in the universe. Use your free will in all your decisions and understand that you're a walking source of God's light, transmitting to others what they need to receive. Use this pure energy to help you with your own life, bringing your life into greater balance and harmony. Through the channeling work, find that not only are you obtaining connection with others, but also answers for yourself. If at first the information is a little fuzzy, let it continue coming, let it become more and more focused, let the feelings of joy and well-being increase, and let the harmony with your departed loved ones grow. Let your guides enter your aura gently, but powerfully, for your greater good. Feel the vibratory presence of your teachers as your perception grows, handling this information, beautifully, lightly, and gently. See lights and colors, see faces, as you go into the high levels of dimensions, attracting the highest consciousness, reaching for the highest in the universe; not accepting anything but the highest in your receiving, translating, and expressing.

Receive impressions, filling your head with light and wisdom and expression. Receive energy into your body, mind, and spirit, making you a better channel. Receive God's love, sending it throughout every part of your consciousness. Feel your loved ones' love, feel the wisdom, feel the light come into you, and through you and from you. Feel appreciative of your guardian angels, guides, and loved ones and of the energy that is being given to you. Feel thankful, and always thank the energy and the teachers who have been good enough to work with you. Increase your purpose in life. Let go of ego. Get rid of selfishness. Deal only with God consciousness as we deal with these beings of light, and the language of love. Understand that God truly is love, and we are an expression of that love through our channeling. Remember the importance of prayer, that our prayers are heard and they are answered, in keeping with our own karmic destinies.

If you'd like to continue now, let's go through the process of energizing the chakras with color this time.

Go through the sequence of energizing each chakra again. This time visualize a different color with each chakra to further strengthen our power of visualization and concentration. We'll use the seven natural colors of the visible spectrum as is seen in a rainbow and proceed from the lower frequency of vibration to the higher.

See a ball of red light at the base of your spine as you energize your first chakra, the muladhara chakra, as it is named in Sanskrit. This energy is very physical, very passionate.

Feel energy passing up to the second chakra, behind the navel, which now glows with a beautiful orange light. This chakra is called the swadishtana.

Allow the energy to pass up to the third chakra, in the solar plexus just below the rib cage, called the manipura chakra. This chakra now glows with a brilliant yellow light like sunlight, also called solar prana.

See the energy move up to the heart chakra, called the anahata chakra, which now glows with a soothing, healing green light. Take a moment to send this loving energy to everyone and everything in the universe. Pause quietly for a few seconds and then feel this energy coming back to you from all the universe with unconditional love.

Visualize the energy drifting upward to the throat chakra, the vishudha, which now glows with a beautiful pale blue color. Use this energy to balance and harmonize your thyroid and parathyroid glands. Use it to soothe and heal any throat soreness or vocal chord strain.

See the energy pass up to the third eye, the ajna chakra, between the eyebrows, which then glows with a deep, dark, electrical blue color. This is the color of outer space and angel worlds. Take a moment and let your consciousness extend through the entire cosmos while you feel your kinship with it, your return to your origin.

Finally, allow the energy to drift up to the very top of your head and charge the crown chakra, the sahasrara chakra, which then glows with an intense violet light. Feel the energy projecting upward and connecting you with the ultimate, beyond space and time, with the primal, creative consciousness of the universe, which we call God or Allah or Brahma or Jehovah or other holy name.

Now feel the energy flowing back, down around you, and absorb it into your being. Say, "I am in the infinite energy and the infinite energy is within me."

Continue to sit quietly and listen with your eyes closed. It's good to be looking slightly upward toward your third eye (ajna chakra) to better perceive any clairvoyant (visual) impressions. As you sit quietly, notice how your breathing has become barely perceptible. Allow yourself to go deeper into the silence. There will be a profound stillness around you. Don't go to sleep. Be aware. If you feel you may doze off, this is the time to ask that one or more of your guides or teachers touch base with you.

Continue to just listen. Listen to the voice within, increasing the attunement each time you do this. What impressions are you receiving? Go deeper into the silence within. You are the temple. You are the conduit to those you love and miss. Reach for the God within, and without.

If you are not receiving specific impressions in this session, don't be discouraged. Instead, sit quietly and allow universal energy, spiritual light to gently flow into you. Allow the beings of light to express that light through you, letting these beings offer expression, clarity, or direction, in whatever areas of your life they feel would be necessary. Let the high guides come to light your path. See the light, feel the light, and feel the protection.

One you are ready to stop the session, you should come out as easily as when you began. Start breathing more deeply, awaken, and reconnect with the physical.

My love is with you, and my appreciation that I've had the opportunity of being with you as perhaps a small bit of help along the way.

Om, shanti . . . peace and love with you always.

Remember the words that were spoken by the angel Gabriel,
"For nothing will be impossible with God."

—LUKE 1:37

PART III

Loud and Clear:
Beyond the Seven Steps

Between the people of eternity and the people
of earth, there is a constant communication.
Oftimes an individual will perform an act,
believing that it is born of his own free
will, accord and command, but in fact he is
being guided and impelled with a precision
to do it. Many great people attained their glory by
surrounding themselves in complete submission to
the will of the spirit, as a violin surrenders itself
to the complete will of a fine musician.

—KAHLIL GIBRAN, *WISDOM OF GIBRAN*

ELEVEN

Departed but Not Gone: Further Ways of Contacting Those We Love

God put me on this earth to accomplish a certain
number of things. Right now, I'm so far behind
that I will probably never die.

—ANONYMOUS

In your quest for spirit communication, you may
want to try some other techniques in addition to the ones already
provided. I hope these will be of additional help to you.

Scrying, or Crystal Gazing

Crystal gazing, the use of crystal balls and mirror gazing, is probably the oldest, most relied-upon technique for spirit communication.

A black obsidian stone mirror is an effective tool for spiritual communication. It can be purchased at most metaphysical shops or candle shops.

There's also a spirit-bridging technique known as scrying, which is a form of crystal gazing. It usually involves letting your eyes go slightly out of focus in a semidark room, and tuning in to the pictures or impressions in a glass. It may take years of concentrated effort before experiencing any spirit phenomena. However, when eventually experiencing the incredible visions that can be seen only with glass, crystal, or even obsidian stone, it is always felt that the concentrated time and effort is well worth it. I have one caveat, however. The crystal used should be clear, not milky, contain no bubbles, and preferably not be low-vibe lead crystal. High vibrations are the name of the game when reaching out to the spirit world.

You may also wish to try gazing into an ordinary mirror. Over a period of minutes, hours, or possibly days, you will notice that the mirror becomes cloudy. As that point, you will probably feel heavy all over, in combination with tingling in various parts of your body.

Always begin all intuitive work with a prayer of protection (see Chapter 4, on prayer), and end with an expression of gratitude.

The crystal will often appear hazy or cloudy at first. However, as you relax and your level of consciousness changes, you may gradually "see" images appear, or receive telepathic impressions. These impressions may be fleeting, but hold on to them and they will in time become stronger. Describe your impressions into a tape recorder if you are alone so you may remember them afterward.

Many people, like my friend Connie, have immediate success with the use of a crystal ball. "I was shocked," she reported. "No sooner had I started gazing into the ball did I start seeing faces . . . first, they were hard to see, and then, guess what? I saw a face that looked very much like Dorrie, my young sister who died when she was twelve!"

The basic formula for success in reaching the highest entities in the spirit world, is: The highest energy attracts the highest energy!

If you wish to be eternally happy, know and believe
that you live after death. Always remember this,
for it is the most important truth.

—EMANUEL SWEDENBORG, *HEAVENLY SECRETS*

Throughout history, all cultures have embraced the concept of communication with those who have passed away. Myths such as the Greek story of Demeter and Persephone, and the Egyptian story of Isis and Osiris, remind people that it is possible to reconnect with those who have died.

Present-day aborigines, like their ancestors, rub clean stones together for four to five days in an attempt to gain access to the spirit world. Confucian and Buddhist religions encourage the use of household altars for daily rituals that promote a reciprocal relationship with their deceased ancestors. A recent front-page article in *The New York Times,* entitled "For Rural Japanese, Death Doesn't Break Family Ties," tells of a widow in a rural Japanese village who offers her deceased husband rice every morning at the altar in her home, and holds conversations with him, hearing his responses in her head.

The Therapy of Writing a Letter to a Departed Loved One

If you feel that there were things that were left unsaid before your loved one passed away, you might consider writing a letter. You might even want to write a letter a day, before going to sleep each night. You may want to do this until you feel that there is nothing else that was left unsaid. It may go on for a week, a year or a lifetime! It's great therapy. It will reveal parts of yourself that are in need of nurturing and healing. Your spirit loved one will draw close to you as you are writing the letter, and will undoubtedly be aware of your feelings and the contents of the message. It will be almost impossible not to feel his or her strong presence. It will be very helpful and bonding to both of you.

Here are some topics that you might wish to address:

- What do I regret about our time together?

- What do I miss most of all?

- What would you like me to say or do that was left unsaid or undone?

- Are there any unaddressed issues?

- Is there any cause or need for forgiveness?

- Were we open and honest with each other?

- What did we appreciate most of all about each other?

- Did we express enough love for each other?

- Did we express enough appreciation and kindness for each other?

- What were my mistakes, and how can I make amends?

- Are there any remaining regrets or omissions?

- Are there any messages for those of us who are still here?

Letters that address unresolved issues such as these may well serve to open the lines of communication with departed loved ones. You will hear and feel many of their answers in your heart, head, and in some cases ears, or in your dream state.

Many times, writing a letter to a spirit loved one will open the door to "guided imagery." This may occur with a spontaneous image of the person whom you are trying to contact.

In addition, it is very possible for letters to take on the expression of spirit loved ones through the medium known as "automatic writing." It truly becomes their expression, rather than yours. Of course, it can also be mutual.

A good way to begin this type of communication is with any of the above questions.

It is a far, far better thing that I do, than anything
I have ever done; it is a far, far better rest that
I go to than I have ever known.

—Charles Dickens

Apologies from Heaven

Forgiveness is very important! Many spirits have communicated about lack of forgiveness. When this occurs they can get stuck and can't seem to go higher in God's kingdom until they are forgiven for their deeds, or they forgive those who hurt them.

I recently was contacted by Leonard Liebman, a psychic medium friend in Florida. While I was having a phone conversation with him, he suddenly stopped midsentence. He said, "Wait a second . . . David Susskind is here." David Susskind, you may remember, was a famous television host who passed away a few years ago. He continued, "David is asking for your forgiveness for a something that he did that hurt you. He says he can't go on until you forgive him. He says you'll know what he's talking about!"

I was shocked. I had never told anyone about my brief encounter with David Susskind. I couldn't believe that he was now asking me for forgiveness. At the time the incident occurred, it was annoying, but I forgot about it. All it involved was that I was called to audition for a guest spot on his show during a bad blizzard. I entered the interview room, which was filled with other wanna-be guests. David was at one end, and I was all the way at the other end, by the door. As producers asked questions, we were supposed to shout out answers! I couldn't and wouldn't do it. Of course, I wasn't chosen to be on the show. I didn't think it was fair, but so many worse things have happened to all of us. Apparently, though, it was in some karmic corner of David's universal consciousness, and the air had to be cleared.

I laughed, and said to Leonard, "Please tell David that there's no need for an apology, but that the apology is accepted if it is helpful to him. Tell him to enjoy his divine existence."

Wow. An astral apology from David Susskind. Now I've heard everything!

The point is that we can't go on in God's universe if there are unresolved or forgiveness issues. It's far easier to do while we're on earth and have physical bodies. When we need to ask someone we've hurt for forgiveness, it's easier to do it by phone, mail, or e-mail, than from the other side.

The Holy Spirit and Our Departed Loved Ones

The Holy Spirit is recognized by most formal religions, but has many different names. For instance, American Indians referred to it as "the Great Spirit." The Holy Spirit is the expression of God's power and intelligence. It is a mystical force within our consciousness that keeps us always aware and mindful of God. As the voice for God, the Holy Spirit lovingly reminds us of the God-mind connection within ourselves.

Through meditation and prayer, the Holy Spirit can inspire us. It allows a free flow of messages and information from God and our highest spirit teachers.

Frequently, when we feel blocked and spirit communication seems difficult or impossible, we should do the following: Ask in prayer for the Holy Spirit to open the lines of spirit communication for us. Ask that it be done smoothly, safely, and easily. We want contact and communication, but it is natural to be afraid. In most cases, it's a new, possibly frightening experience. Therefore, we will ask the Holy Spirit to help us. Your religious background doesn't matter. Ask in prayer for "a blanket of light and protection" to surround and guide you. Know in your heart, mind, and spirit that these will be safe, wonderful spiritual experiences.

And He shall wipe away all tears from their eyes;
And there shall be no more death,
Neither sorrow, nor crying,
Neither shall there be any more pain;
For the former things are passed away.

—REV., 21:4

TWELVE

Communication: A Two-Way Process

Invention is the most important product of man's
creative brain. The ultimate purpose is the complete
mastery of mind over the material world, the
harnessing of human nature to human needs.

—NIKOLA TESLA

As you know by now, contact can begin in the
most gentle, barely perceptible of ways. Contact also occurs in the
most amazing of ways. While contact is generally the result of
heartfelt and dedicated attempts to reach someone, it can appear
to be spontaneous, with seemingly no initiation on the part of the
receiving party. By opening your receptivity through the Seven
Steps, centering yourself, and requesting that contact be made,

"spontaneous" communication will undoubtedly occur regularly on its own.

I offer the following additional ways of contact so you will not overlook what might be subtle, or unique, methods of communication.

Spirit Gifts

Have you ever had anything appear from out of nowhere? Maybe it was just a feather, or perhaps an earring. The most common spirit gift is a coin. It can be just a penny, but it seems to appear from out of nowhere and somehow presents itself very clearly to you. Many times our spirit guides and teachers bring us an object that is powerfully "charged" with energy that we need for a particular experience or phase of our lives.

When an object comes from the world of spirit, it is called an "apport" (a'-port). Most apports are considered to be "evanescent," which means they were brought from the spirit world, and after a short period of time will go back to that world. In other words, they disappear! Throughout my life, I have found earrings and things that I couldn't explain, while losing things that were in their place. The Native American spirit teacher at Silver Bell often presented participants in the séances with little gifts and photos. Arrowheads are a favorite apport given to us by our Native American guides, but all guides like to give apports as a connecting link to help us focus our energy, whether it's for basic meditation, spirit connection, healing, or other uplifting purposes.

Over the years, I have received many apport gifts. I received one of my favorites, a necklace with blue stones, at a séance in Pennsylvania. A medium brought it to me through a "trumpet," which is just what it sounds like: a large tubular-shaped horn that the medium holds up to receive the apport. I put on the necklace and went home. It was quite late and I tiptoed into my bedroom. Not wanting to disturb my husband, I did not turn on the light. Jack woke up anyway, saw me, and in the dark bedroom said, "What's that thing that's glowing?" We looked at my new present together. It was made with simple blue stones and had a beautiful spirit light. After about ten years, the necklace disappeared. I knew that it had returned to the world of spirit— it was evanescent.

Other gifts I or members of my family have received include bracelets, rings, packages of spices, photos, and once, a beautiful old pair of shoes. Usually, these have disappeared within a period of time, after the receiver was "finished" with needing them.

Electronic Voice Phenomena (EVP) and Instrumental Transcommunication (ITC)

In the twentieth and twenty-first centuries, amazing technological advances have been made that involve spirit contact. In the past, spirits have resorted to conveying messages in such methods as tea leaves, while today a whole array of high-tech avenues exists. These technologies are the New Age answer to old methods of spirit contact, and in my estimation, are destined to make séances look passé.

Electronic voice phenomena (EVP) is the process whereby voices of the departed become embedded in electronic recording equipment, resulting in a recorded voice or transmitted message. While EVP is the term used to describe electronic voice phenomena, the term instrumental transcommunication (ITC) describes images. There has been much success lately with both EVP and ITC. Messages have been received from departed loved ones through tape recorders, VCRs, televisions, telephones, and even computers. The spirit world has entered the electronic age!

Television

In 1985, German metaphysician Klaus Schreiber started receiving pictures of deceased family members on his home television. Sometimes just one voice would come across telling Schreiber how to tune his TV for better reception. When Schreiber passed away soon after, his own image began to show up on the TV screens of some European ITC researchers.

Telephone

In 1996, ITC researcher Adolph Homes received a series of paranormal phone calls from his deceased mother. "Adolph, this is your mother. I'm going to contact you several times by phone. It may be difficult to understand me at times, since my thoughts will be transmitted to you with different patterns. Your vibrational work with equipment makes these contacts possible."

Computer

Can departed entities make contact through computers? Yes, they can, according a number of German researchers. One researcher received a spontaneous message that appeared first as a series of letters, then words, and finally phrases that referred clearly to a deceased friend of the investigator. Four years later, an English professor claimed to have exchanged messages by e-mail for more than fifteen months with a group of advanced entities living in the year 2019, as well as a man from the year 1546.

According to the Association of Electronic Voice Phenomena, the following characteristics have been identified by EVP experimenters:

- More messages are recorded at night or during stormy weather than during the day or when the weather is clear.

- EVP message length is typically very short, ranging from one word to short sentences. Messages will usually be less than two seconds in duration.

Popular theories for why this is so include:

- There may be a limit to the amount of EVP information that can be transmitted in a single message.

- The energy required for transmission of messages is limited by available physical energy, such as that provided by sound, electricity, or light.

- The experimenter's personal mediumistic ability is a limiting factor for message length.

- EVP messages are usually relevant to the person doing the recording. Cross correspondence, in which two or more experimenters receive similar messages, has occurred, but this is not common. Personally relevant messages are received, even when a group of people record together with individual recording apparatus.

Reverse Messages

Messages are often found by listening to the reverse direction of a soundtrack. When audiotape is used, the tape is played in the reverse so that the experimenter's voice is heard as reverse gibberish but entity words are clearly heard as if played in the correct direction. When a computer-based sound editor is used as an audio recorder, playing the sound file in the reverse mode will often disclose messages.

Explanations for the existence of reverse messages include:

- The entities experience a different time frame from us; thus they are able to impress messages in either direction in our time frame.

- Most EVP recording is done in a sound-rich environment. Most recording situations have some amount of echo or reverberate, even if it is not obvious to the casual observer. Reverse voices may be made possible by the echoed sound.

Invocation

Asking the entities to communicate at the beginning of a recording session has been found to substantially increase the level of contact.

Audibly speaking the invocation and questions during a recording session is more effective than doing so mentally.

Scheduled Sessions

At least for new experimenters, recording at the same time of day and week results in more messages than choosing random recording times. At least one researcher has determined that this effect diminishes as the experimenter gains experience.

Audiotape

Two pioneers of EVP were Konstantin Raudive and Fredrich Juergenson, both Swedes. In the mid 1900s Mr. Raudive heard words recorded on blank audiotape and eventually made more than ten thousand recordings. Juergenson captured voices while taping bird songs outdoors. His research continued for twenty-five years.

Belling and Lee, a British laboratory, conducted some experiments on EVP, suspecting that the spirit voices were caused by ham radio broadcasting bouncing off the ionosphere. The tests were conducted by one of the leading sound engineers in Britain, and when phantom voices were recorded on factory-fresh tape, he was baffled. Lee is quoted as saying, "I cannot explain what happened in normal physical terms."

In 1952, two Italian Catholic priests were trying to record a Gregorian chant but had difficulty when a wire in their equipment kept breaking. Out of desperation, one of the priests called on his deceased father for help. To his shock, his father's voice was clearly heard on the tape saying, "I'm here son. Of course I will help you. I'm always with you." The priests brought the matter to the attention of Pope Pius XII, who reportedly accepted the authenticity of the phenomenon.

By the end of the 1980s, throughout Europe, North America, South America, and Asia, thousands reported receiving messages from entities claiming to be spiritual beings who had once existed in human form on the earth.

When I tried electronic spirit contact with my reel-to-reel tape recorder, I had intriguing results. I set up the recorder in a quiet room, and let it run during the night for a number of nights. During the day, I played the tape. The tape from the third night had the sound of beginning of words. By the seventh night, words and sentences were forming, and with some difficulty, I was able to discern, "I g-r-e-e-e-t y-o-o-u . . ." It is an intriguing experiment. But, I didn't have the patience to pursue it after that. Perhaps it will be faster and easier for you.

Radio

In 1990, two research teams, one in the United States and one in Germany, independently developed devices that allowed them to speak to the dead. Using their own version of a ham radio that receives up to fourteen different frequencies at once, the researchers claimed to have held conversations with at least five deceased people. Dr. Ernst Senkowski, in Germany, said that he contacted a German shipman who died in 1965. Dr. Senkowski said, "We verified the information. He told us he was doing well, and was happy." In the United States, George Meek, director of the Metascience Foundation in Franklin, North Carolina, said that he has spoken more than twenty-five times to Dr. George J. Mueller, an electrical engineer who died in 1967 of heart failure. "Dr. Mueller told us where to find his birth and death certificate records," along with other details, Meek reported. The bottom line is that it was all confirmed as being true.

You might try using a tape recorder, a pair of headphones, a microphone, a jack plug and lead, and a radio. First, plug one end of the jack plug into the recorder and the other end into the radio. Turn the radio onto a static station, which will prevent other stations from being mistaken as spirit voices. The radio will create background noise. The jack plug and lead also make sure that no radio noise is recorded except for the sound of communication from the spirit world. Plug the headphones and the microphones into the recorder and hit "record." Have a short pause, and then introduce yourself to your spirit friends. Ask them to communicate with you, and tell them that you are not a negative or harmful presence. This information is outlined in the book *Mysteries of the Unexplained* by H. G. Carlson (see the Resources section).

> *Every living being is an engine geared*
> *to the wheelwork of the universe.*
>
> —NIKOLA TESLA

White Noise

With the introduction of relaxing sound machines that play everything from thunderstorms to rushing waterfalls, the phenomenon of white noise has recently been recognized as a successful tool for spirit contact. Even *Scientific American* has recognized white noise as a successful tool for spirit contact. Its technical name is "stochastic resonance."

White noise can be effective for spirit contact and often works quickly. What usually occurs is that as you listen to the white noise, you "go into the sound" and relax deeply. As this occurs, spirit voices can sometimes be heard. Perhaps at first it's just a whisper, then words become more clearly formed, eventually becoming recognizable sentences. When I tried it, it took me about four attempts to obtain results. The first word I heard was from my mother, who very clearly said, "Joy . . . Joy." She always called me Joy!

Spirit Photography

Many people make a big deal out of spirit photography. In reality, nothing could be easier. In my experience the best spirit photography is done without a flash. Many people have found results with 200 ASA or 400 ASA Kodak Gold film. For me, I prefer a simple Polaroid or any inexpensive camera.

In the beginning, a lot of spirit photography simply shows up as a light, a streak, or a blob of light. Eventually, you may start to see small faces in your photos—faces of people whom you know were not physically there.

I have been fortunate to receive many wonderful spirit photographs. Some were taken with Polaroid cameras, others with 35mm cameras (see photos). The type of film and camera doesn't seem to be that significant, as spirit phenomena can appear in a variety of ways, and taken with almost any type of camera and film.

Photographs of the author on *The Richard Bey Show,* with colored spirit light streaks in both shots. (Photographs by Jack Keller)

Sometimes, the most amazing spirit photo can be a huge white light that appears over a person's head.

As in the case of the aforementioned picture of Mataji, I have received many amazing spirit photos at spirit circles. I received a

photo of a baby that I miscarried twelve years earlier. Seen next to a real photo of my husband, Jack, such as one taken when he was approximately the same age, they look like twins! Obviously, babies and children who cross over continue to grow in the spirit world.

I have also received spirit photos of my spirit guides, teachers, and relatives. An example of impressive proof is the spirit photo of my grandfather, who looks very much like the physical photo that was taken before he passed away.

Spirit photograph of the author's miscarried daughter from the mediumistic circle at Silver Belle, in Ephrata, Pennsylvania. (Imprinted on fabric; Photograph by Jack Keller)

Can you do this yourself? Absolutely. I have found that many photos contain spirit manifestation in a way that is usually ignored. It may be thought to be an imperfect picture, when really it's a flash of spirit light and a greeting from the spirit world. If you look closely at photos that you have taken over the years, you may be surprised to find faces where they don't belong, or perhaps someone standing in a family photo, when you know that that person was not physically there.

Author's husband, Jack Keller, high school graduation photo, for comparison with photo above.

Many people enjoy going to cemeteries and taking pictures of graves and tombstones. This could be very intriguing, and surprising. A warning, though. Results don't always happen on the first attempt. You may have to repeat the effort a number of times. It speeds up the process if you ask your spirit guides, friends, and teachers to show their faces on your film.

If you choose to try spirit photography in a cemetery, choose one that is old, with some history behind it and a buildup of vibrations. Speak softly. Walk around the cemetery for thirty to forty minutes to allow the spirits to adjust to you. Try taking photos in cemeteries just as it is growing dark. Stay positive; expect some manifestation.

No, spirits will not follow you home, nor will you be in danger from these spirit entities. When you are ready to leave, thank them for cooperating, and tell the spirits that they should go "into the light," and should not go home with you. They will listen and respect your wishes.

On a technical note, flash cameras usually work best in cemeteries. APS cameras and digital cameras work well. Many people have had results with 35mm and APS cameras, and with the NV-323 Night Vision Scope. The following

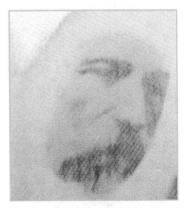

Spirit photograph of the author's grandfather from the mediumistic circle at Silver Belle in Ephrata, Pennsylvania. (Imprinted on fabric; photograph by Jack Keller)

Actual photograph of author's grandfather taken around 1900, for comparison with spirit photograph.

cameras have also been reported effective for graveyard spirit photography:

- Casio QV700

- Sony Mavica FD-7

- Olympus D-220L

- Kodak DC 210

If it is too cold out, you might actually be photographing your own breath. Keep the camera strap out of the way, and away from the lens. Keep free-flowing hair and fingers away from the lens as well.

Those who have crossed over really want us to know that there is life after death. Spirit friends and loved ones are very happy to have the opportunity of communicating with us. Sometimes though, especially when electronic equipment is used, quite a bit of patience and time may be involved before successful results are manifested. Don't give up!

A Little Story About God and the Scientist

A scientist approached God and said, listen, we've decided that we no longer need you. Nowadays, we can clone people, transplant hearts, and do all kinds of things that were once considered miraculous. God patiently listened and then said, "All right. To see whether or not you still need me, why don't we have a man-making contest?" The scientist agreed. "Now, we're going to do this just like I did back in the old days with Adam," God said. "That's fine," replied the scientist as he bent to scoop up a handful of dirt. "Whoa!" God said, shaking his head in disapproval. "Not so fast, pal. You get your own dirt."

THIRTEEN

A Final Communication

There is no death! What seems so is actually transition.

This life of mortal breath is but a suburb of the life elysian,

whose portal is what we call death.

—HENRY WADSWORTH LONGFELLOW

As you know, the purpose of this book is to help you contact those you've loved and lost by offering a concrete system for tuning in and connecting. But the ways of spirit are not always concrete, and their messages are not always understandable or welcome. Yet they are never given to us without at least our subconscious permission, or before we are ready to hear. Almost always, however, contact is made for our welfare. I relate the following experiences not as examples of what will happen if you follow one or more of the techniques given in a haphazard way, but rather, when incorporated into a daily and dedicated pattern for living—complete with positive lifestyle choices—how you may then become a continual feed of information with the other side. Our loved ones, angels, and spirit guides are with us always, and readily answer our calls for help when necessary, and will answer our desire for contact when requested. As the examples below demonstrate, they will also supply you with answers before you even know that your family or you need them.

Jerry had gone down his street thousands of times on his way home. As he attempted to turn his compact car down the street, the wheel suddenly wouldn't turn. Angry, he shook the steering wheel of the car. Then he clearly heard a familiar voice say, "Jerry, just let the car go." He was forced to continue driving straight rather than turning in the direction of his house, due to the immobilized wheel. He no sooner had driven past the street when a huge gasoline truck came barreling along the street at full speed, headed the wrong way along this one-way street. At that moment he realized the voice he heard was his grandfather's, who had passed on years prior. Jerry would have been part of a major fireball had his grandfather not intervened.

Ellen and Maggie were about to have lunch in a diner. As Ellen's hamburger was served to her, she heard her departed sister, Janet's, voice. Janet said twice, "Don't eat that!"

Ellen was shocked, since she had not heard Janet's voice since before she passed away months earlier. She was about to bite into the burger anyway when she heard the voice again. This time, it was much louder. Ellen did not ignore it this time.

She opened the bun on the burger. To her shock, she found a small, but strong, coiled metal wire. She said an appreciative thank-you to her dear sister, Janet, then, of course, called for the waitress.

Paula and her husband were in a great financial bind and in need of a hundred dollars to pay a bill. While she and her husband, Tom, were sleeping, Paula was roused to a semiawake state and saw a magnificent vision of her departed mother. She was completely awestruck. The spirit was completely bathed in a blue, glowing light.

The apparition said softly and sweetly, "Paula ... when you awaken, you will find the money that you need on the dresser, under Mother Mary's statue. To prove that you are not dreaming this, I will twist the head ever so slightly on this statue." Then, she added, "One warning, though. You must spend the money. If you try to save it, it will go back to the spirit world." Paula then fell into a deep sleep.

The next morning, Paula tried to explain to her husband what had happened during the night and showed him the money. He laughed a little, and said incredulously, "People come in the night and *take* money. No one brings it!"

Paula then pointed to the unusual angle of the statue's neck. Paula and Tom both acknowledged that something extraordinary had occurred.

When Julie, one of our regular listeners, called in, she related the following incident: She and her sister Sylvie were sitting in a dark movie theater, giggling, watching a movie and having fun.

Julie pulled out a box of cheese crackers from a brown paper bag. She opened the box and reached in to take a cracker. She was surprised to suddenly feel an unseen hand grip hers!

"Joyce," she reported, "I was sure that I was imaging things. I tried again to take one, but met with strong physical resistance. I was so intrigued, that I crawled over my sister and everyone else in the row of seats. I walked right to the lighted part of the theater."

"I let out a loud 'Yikes!' The box was crawling with roaches! I would have gone back to my seat," she added, "to offer them to my sister, but I was too busy screaming!"

Two years after Barry lost his wife, Tracy, he married a woman named Jill. The first night Barry and his new bride slept in their new home, Barry awoke during the night. He caught a quick glimpse of his first wife, sweetly smiling at the foot of his bed. The next morning, when he awoke, he realized that his new wife's picture was facing down on his dresser. Nothing occurred after that, but the message from Tracy was clear!

• • •

Terry reported a visitation from her recently departed, beloved dog, Rubie. Rubie let her owner know that she was fine and relaxing in a pet hospital bed. Not only that, but the railings were pulled up, so she wouldn't fall out of bed. Terry reported, "I felt Rubie lick my face, just like old times!"

As for stories about pets, here are a couple of my own.

After our thirteen-year-old cat, Sydney, passed into cat heaven, he came to me several times in dreams and meditation. He spoke to me in beautiful, clear English and wanted us to know that he was doing well. This was a cat with a sense of humor. In life, he had been a rust-colored calico with a large amount of white fur on the front of his body. In his first communication with me after crossing over, he said, "Mommy, don't be sad. Look at me. Look at my fur. It's still white!" That was an inside joke, because when he was in his body, he would speak to me telepathically and slyly say that he was not rust-colored but white, because that was the color on the front of his body that he could see. He certainly hadn't changed after his passing.

We had an old dog named Jim who had psychiatric problems. No matter how we tried to lift his spirits, he was always depressed and withdrawn. After his crossing, he didn't communicate with me. I just saw him curled in a ball and withdrawn into a corner. Just like when he was in a physical body. As in his physical life, he still seemed to be in his own world.

When our dog Ben crossed over after a long illness, however, he came to me the first night after his passing. This dog had always been more human than canine. He was lying in what looked like a small-sized hospital bed. He raised his head, and said, "Hey, look at me! They tell me I'm going to be just fine. I love you and Dad and miss you guys. Don't be sad! Thank you for everything. I especially enjoyed those meals of people food." Then he put his head down and went back to sleep.

The veil that separates the worlds is but a thin veil.
For those who purify their hearts by faith,

the veil is rolled aside, and they can see and
know that death is an elusive thing.

—The Aquarian Gospel

I could relate dozens more of these and my own communication experiences, but will limit myself to a few more for the purpose of uncovering the deeper meaning often found in spirit messages.

Jack and I had been unsuccessfully searching for a house. We were starting to feel that our search was fruitless. We felt that we would never find a house that we loved at a price we could afford, in a neighborhood that we wanted.

I asked my spirit loved ones to help us, and they did. In meditation, they showed me a ranch house, gave me the numbers 168, and said it was on the street behind Sears Department Store.

When I drove down the street behind Sears, there was no number 168. As I drove farther, however, I found a For Sale sign on a house. The number was 1068! Close enough. I didn't exactly love it from the outside. Nonetheless, I called the phone number on the sign. The previous owners had died, and the real estate agency was eager to make a sale. We bought it, and lived in that house for ten happy years.

I believe the message here is to stay open to possibilities.

Interpreting spirit messages is not always easy, or clear, as you will see from the following.

One day I received a phone call from one of my radio-show listeners who was very upset. She said, "Joyce, my father has Alzheimer's. He wandered out of an open door in our home, and he's missing. Can you help?"

While she was speaking, I started seeing palm trees. I very distinctly heard one of my spirit loved ones say, "He's in Florida!" I closed my eyes and saw an elderly gentleman sitting on a park bench in a busy place.

I asked the woman, "Could he be in Florida? Do you think he might be sitting on a park bench in a busy place?"

She was silent, and then said, "How could he have gotten all the way to Florida from New York?" She added disappointedly, "Oh, I'll get back to you. Thanks."

The tone of her voice made me sad, yet I felt that the information had been correct.

The next day, the woman called, excited. She said, "Joyce, you'll never believe this. When I told my husband what you had said, he asked, 'Didn't your father have old cronies in upstate New York? In fact, isn't there a town called Florida, near the town where he lived?'"

Well, they went to the town of Florida, New York, which I had never heard of, went to a bus depot, and found the confused father sitting on a bench.

I feel the lesson here is to listen to that still, small voice within. Spirit teachers and loved ones want to help us.

On another occasion my daughter Elaine, who was attending New York University, called me and said, "Mom, you have to come get me. I'm sick. I think I'm having an appendicitis attack."

I raced into Manhattan and found her in great pain. I took her to the hospital where it was determined that she should have her appendix removed. While I waited alone with her in a little examining room, I realized that I had not yet asked in prayer for her to be healed without surgery.

I placed my hands over her head. I felt the presence of a spirit loved one who directed me to sweep my arms over the full length of her body, and to do that three times. As I was doing this, I looked up at a white curtain hanging near her bed and saw the full outline of a Native American! Of course, there was no one physically there but us. The good news is that moments after that occurred, she sat up in bed and was fine. She was dismissed about an hour later.

Once again I say, prayers are heard, and often bring about miracles.

When I was about fourteen, I was sleeping deeply in my cozy warm bed on a cold winter night. Softly, a little voice called me and said, "Joyce, get up. Get up, now." I continued to sleep, ignoring the voice.

The voice grew louder, "Joyce, please, get up now!" I reluctantly opened one eye. When I didn't see anyone there, I went back to sleep.

The third time, the voice was so loud that I shot straight up. "Joyce, get up, now!"

Even though I couldn't see anything, I realized that an angel was speaking to me. The voice continued, "Stand up. You have to go down to the basement."

The basement! I didn't go down to the basement even on a warm, sunny day. It was a dark, cold, damp and spooky night. Why should I go now?

I clearly heard the angel say, "Don't worry, I'll go first."

Quietly, not wanting to disturb my family, I tiptoed to the top of the basement stairs. I took a deep breath, turned on the light, and gingerly descended the squeaky stairs. As I got close to the base of the stairway, I smelled smoke.

The smell was coming from an oily rag, which was starting to smolder. It was draped over a pipe, which was directly over the oil burner. I grabbed the rag and ran upstairs with it. I threw it in some dirt near the front door.

When I told my father about it the next day, he said, "We received an oil delivery yesterday. The deliveryman must have left that rag there! But, wait, how did you know about it? You never go in the basement."

When I told him, he remarked that I was becoming just like my mother.

I feel the message here that those in spirit want to help us. It's up to us to listen. And here is the most amazing story of all.

God's Portal

During July 2001, Jack and I fell in love with an apartment in the shadow of the World Trade Center. It was an amazing apartment, on the thirty-sixth floor, with sweeping views of the New York Harbor and the Statue of Liberty. Half of the roof of the building looked out onto the harbor. The other half had an overwhelming view of the World Trade Center. Even though I had negative feelings about the area, there was no way that we could not buy this apartment. It was perfect for us; we loved everything about it.

Everything was made easy for us. The purchase of the apartment and moving in went more quickly and smoothly than any transaction in which we had ever before partaken. It was all done within a period of two weeks. Jack and I were amazed.

We just about finished moving in by September 9. We left on Sunday to attend a christening on Long Island and we were not in the city on September 11, the day of the terrorist attacks.

A few days after 9/11 we returned to the apartment, which was, amazingly, untouched. The doorman hugged us in an expression of grief and relief. The first night back in the apartment, soon after falling asleep, I was abruptly awakened. I couldn't see anything. The room seemed to be filled with choking smoke . . . I was screaming, crying, sweating, and unable to see anything. I was hysterical and terrified. I ran screaming into the living room, feeling as if my chest and head were being crushed. There was no air to breathe. Clearly, I was dying.

After a few moments I was able to see through the dust and rubble, and I began to see firemen. They extended their arms and picks, along with other instruments, toward me. One of them told me, "We're here to help lead these people out of this." I realized that they didn't know that they were dead.

One of my spirit teachers, Earlyne, appeared, and spoke softly to me. She said, "You and Jack have been brought here for a job. A portal, or doorway, has been created by the spirit world in this living room window." She continued, "It is your job to help to lead these departed folks out through this portal and out into the light." She pointed out the window toward a bright light in the middle of the harbor, to the right of the Statue of Liberty. I had never seen that light before. It was warm, welcoming, and it softly glowed over the harbor.

By now, Jack was up and standing next to me. Earlyne directed Jack and me to stand in front of the window, facing each other, about five feet apart, arms extended from our sides. We were told by

Earlyne that the spirit world not only needed our physical presence, but also the sound of our voices. We were asked to repeat as we guided the departed souls out the window, "Go into the light! Look for the light over the harbor! Go toward the light. Go into the light! Don't be afraid. God loves you! You are safe now. Go into the light!"

We repeated this over and over, and said prayers that we felt would be helpful. The room seemed to be filled with firemen, policemen, men, and women. Some left quickly and easily. Some were happy and glad to go. Others were crying and confused. One departed fellow cried, "But I have to go back to my desk!" A spirit teacher took him by the hand and led him out through the portal.

A fireman made us laugh. He said, "Look, I can fly with my boots on!" He left easily and joyfully. Many of these departed folks did not know what had happened and did not know where they were. There was a feeling, though, of understanding, accept-ance, and resignation. I was told to tell them that things would be better for them, and more joyful, after they entered the light.

Many asked where they were. Some asked, "Why can't I see my wife?" "Why can't I see my children?" "Where's my husband?"

There were many confused souls and many questions. We

Photograph of "portal" window in the author's Battery Park City apartment. (Photograph by Jack Keller)

kept telling them, "All will be well. Go into the light! Go with God! Soon all with be explained and understood." "Look for, and follow the light."

They streamed faster and faster by us, as if the word was out and the path had been made easier for them.

As the sun started to come up over the harbor, I realized how fatigued Jack and I were. We had to go to sleep. One of our spirit teachers nodded in our direction. He indicated that we were finished for the time being. I repeated to the departing entities, "Go with God."

We realized that we had been standing by the window for more than four hours, and were soaking wet from perspiration. Earlyne told us, "Don't worry. The vibration has been set up and is established. The work will continue. The portal has been established and will remain active until the job is finished. All is well. Go to sleep."

Since that night, we have made efforts to spiritually cleanse every square inch of the apartment with incense and Indian smudge. We have asked the most spiritual people we know to

Poster of lower Manhattan, purchased after September 11, 2001, photographed by Jack Keller in January 2002. (Publisher of photo unknown)

come and visit us. I know that their presence will help to raise and keep the vibrations as high as possible, both in our apartment and in Battery Park City.

I don't know if this apartment is the only portal that was created for the purpose of guiding souls into the light. I only know that it is a gateway to heaven.

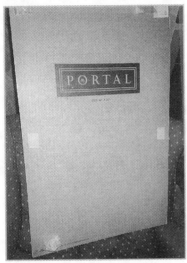

Back side of mounted poster of lower Manhattan, diplaying the word PORTAL.

A few days after this astounding experience, Jack and I were walking on the street near Ground Zero. The air was filled with the acrid smell that emanated from the smoldering pit. Our eyes teared, and our noses burned. Wearing a mask didn't help much.

The streets were filled with tourists. They walked slowly along with people who were in various stages of grief and shock.

There were many street vendors attempting to capitalize on the tragedy. Their wares included photos that were taken in the area of the tragedy, both before and after.

One photo caught my eye. It clearly showed our apartment house in the shadow of the World Trade Center. There was something else about it that I couldn't quite define. It was a beautiful clear photo and it showed everything in such great detail. Of course we bought it.

When we returned home and attempted to mount the photo on the wall, we noticed the back side of the print. Even though it had been photographed well before 9/11, it said in very large letters, "Portal."

Reach Out

Reach out
I'm as close as your hand
Even if you can't see me
In God's heavenly land.

Reach out
Just call my name
I'm hard to see
But my love is the same.

Reach out
Lose the fears
We can connect;
Please dry your tears.

Reach out
Though we're apart
Go on with your life
I'm in your heart.
                    —JOYCE KELLER

A Further Message About the World Trade Center

I hope that relaying these incidents causes no one duress or sadness. But I believe it would be foolhardy not to address the topic that may be the pivotal moment of our century, lifetimes, and perhaps of the Western world. 9/11 is a critical topic concerning why we are here and what we are meant to experience. The event has changed us in ways that are incalculable; its lasting effects are large and wide and to a great extent still completely unknown.

Four months after 9/11, to the very day, I channeled a communication about the destruction of the World Trade Center. I will include its primary message here.

Information comes to us from the spirit plane in a variety of ways and forms we can not always fathom. Nor can we always censor the information that comes to us from these higher sources. Departed loved ones and teachers give us information they wish for us to have, and in some cases to disseminate. This is one of those cases.

The Message:

People who were taken have accelerated their own soul's growth in a way that is not possible for those living in physical bodies. The growth of the people of the planet is also now accelerated as a result of their sacrifice and the psychic shock caused by this event. Millions of people on the planet had their lives changed in an instant when their heart centers were suddenly opened and touched. In many cases, these were people whose emotions had become blocked. This event gave them the opportunity for spiritual opening and renewal.

The saving grace for the planet, which may keep us from destruction, is the love and awareness of the needs of our brothers and sisters around the world. When confronted with evil, and this has always been the greatest challenge for mankind, it is best dealt with by the elevation of human consciousness and the calling upon of the highest energy in the universe, which to many is, of course, God.

I hope this book and these messages have been of support and inspiration to you. Remember always that help is there when your heart seeks it, and contact will be made if your heart desires it.

Trust in the Lord, and do good; so shalt thou dwell
in the land and verily thou shalt be fed.
Delight thyself also in the Lord;
and he shall give thee the desires of thine heart.

—Psalms 37: 3, 4

Glossary

ADC: After-death communication; when loved ones contact us directly after they have passed on.

akashic record: Records the deeds of the soul in all an individual's incarnations.

alpha state: State of brain activity resembling a light trance, the condition one experiences during meditation.

angel: Invisible entities or beings who are with us from lifetime to lifetime.

apports: Evanescent gift from the spirit world.

ascended and universal master teachers: The highest, most evolved teachers. In service to mankind, they will come when they are called.

astral body: Known also as the ethereal body, the unseen counterpart to the physical body.

astral plane: Where most souls exist after death.

attachments: Spirits exerting negative influence.

aural ADC: Hearing a departed one speak to you.

auric shield, aura, or energy field: Semi-invisible extension extending from individuals that protects and insulates.

automatic writing: When a spirit communicates by directing a person's writing.

cosmic consciousness (same as God consciousness): Through deep meditation, an advanced state of awareness wherein we realize the connection of ourselves with all things throughout the universe as if we were God, and in fact, are in a state of oneness or integration with our creator.

business guide: Teacher who helps people know and understand their greatest financial success, in keeping with their personal karma.

chakras: The seven nonphysical centers, or invisible "wheels" that run from the base of the spine to the top of the head.

channeling: Transmitting information from the other side of the veil.

chemist or pharmacist guide: Guide who works primarily with the body chemistry of people who will be doing trance or mediumistic work.

clairaudience: The ability to hear spirits.

clairsentience: The ability to sense the presence of spirit.

clairvoyance: The ability to see spirits.

doctor teacher or guide: Spirit teacher who communicates information about healing.

doorkeeper: Protective force assigned to each individual.

dream incubation: Process in which a person directs the content of his dreams.

ectoplasm: Barely visible substance that emanates from spirits.

enlightenment of the soul: Also known as universal consciousness, or knowing God.

entities: Nonphysical beings.

ethereal body: Also known as the astral body, the spiritual counterpart to the physical body.

ethers: Nonphysical atmosphere that extends throughout the universe and through which consciousness is transmitted.

evanescent: A substance that materializes, or becomes solid, upon entering the physical plane. It will in time return to the nonphysical state.

EVP: Electronic voice phenomena, when spirits' voices are recorded.

fifth chakra: Corresponds with the throat, represents speech and communication.

fourth chakra: Corresponds with the heart, and is exactly where the heart is. Corresponds with love, human feeling, and emotion.

fragrant ADC: When you smell your departed loved one.

gazing: The process of staring at an object for the purpose of connecting with spirit.

ghosts: Earthbound spirits, who have not gone into the light.

God awareness: Oneness with the creator.

God center: That point within us where we perceive our deepest, most quiet and most highly concentrated energy.

God consciousness: Known also as cosmic consciousness, the state in which a person, through meditation, can comprehend the infinity of creation.

higher planes: Developed stages of evolution beyond earth.

hypnagogic state: Drowsy state immediately preceding sleep.

incarnation: Physical lifetime.

Indian guide: Native American spirit who specializes in teaching about nature and natural healing methods. He is a protector and guide in the literal sense of the word.

joy guide: The guide that keeps people laughing and smiling.

karma: The universal law of what you sow, shall ye reap (or, cause and effect) that carries over lifetime to lifetime.

kundalini: The psychic energy that lies dormant at the base of the spine, a very dynamic vital power.

mantra: An affirmation that vibrates at the highest possible frequency.

master teacher: Guide who provides spiritual wisdom and philosophical teachings. Our primary spirit teacher, who usually does not change.

muse or inspiration guide: Guide who inspires and directs creativity.

meditation: The stilling of the conscious mind.

medium: Psychic individual able to connect human beings with nonphysical entities.

meridians: According to Chinese medicine, the fifty-seven invisible energy pathways that run completely around the body, from head to toe, and back up again.

mundane guides: Guides who do the most basic, necessary tasks.

om shanti: Om, or aum, is the primal sound, or the sound of God. Shanti means peace and love.

out-of-body travel: Traveling beyond the limitations of the physical body.

passing over: Known also as moving on or dying, this is physical death.

phenomena: Experiences that cannot be explained in the traditional sense.

photo séances: Silk circles, wherein likenesses appear on silk in a darkened room, representative of those in spirit.

physical plane: Earth.

pierce the bindu: To part the veil between the physical and nonphysical worlds.

power spots: Vortexes where positive energy congregates, such as Sedona, Arizona, or places of worship.

pranayama: Sanskrit term for breath control.

precognition: Perceiving information about the future.

primary teacher or professor guide: Specializes in helping people communicate at peak levels when they are in a teaching capacity.

psychic bugs: Spiritual interference encouraging humans to be involved in negative actions, thoughts, words, or deeds.

psychic: One with a developed extrasensory perception (ESP) that enables him or her to feel, sense, smell, see, or hear that which is not apparent to the five physical senses.

psychometry: Reading impressions left on objects.

root chakra: Located at the base of the spine, corresponds with primal, base energies and expression.

scrying: Divining through such means as a mirror or a crystal ball.

séance: Means of contacting the dead.

second chakra: Corresponds with reproduction, located slightly above the pubic bone, where embryos begin growing.

sentient ADC: A feeling, or a knowing, that a departed loved one is near.

seventh chakra: The crown chakra, found at the top of the head, which goes directly upward to God and the universe.

silver thread: Breaks at the moment of death. Called the "sutratma" in Vedantic teaching and the "life thread" in Western philosophies.

sixth chakra: Corresponds with the third eye, or the spot between and slightly above the eyebrows. Also known as "the eye of God," this chakra controls ESP.

spirit guides: Known also as spirit teachers, these spirits act as bodyguards, protectors, instructors, and connectors.

spirit teachers: Entities who in most cases have incarnated on the earth. They grow in spirit along with us, remembering that for all beings, "The coin of spirit is service."

tangible ADC: When you feel a spirit touch you.

third chakra: Corresponds with the navel or solar plexus chakra, right above the naval, the center of the human body, and the primary life force center.

trance mediumship: Putting consciousness aside and, like a telephone, allowing the nonphysical entity to speak through the medium.

vibration: Level of energy or frequency.

visual ADC: Seeing a departed one.

water: Universal spiritual purifier. Water is a conductor of positive energy, while also being capable of drawing in and holding negative energy.

yoga: Union with God and the divine world of spirit.

Resources

Organizations

Association for Research and Enlightenment
Virginia Beach Headquarters
(757) 428-3588 or (800) 333-4499
215 67th Street, Virginia Beach, VA 23451
www.edgarcayce.org

New York City Branch
(212) 691-7690
150 W. 28th Street, New York, NY 10001
www.mindspring.com/~areofnyc
Additional centers in the United States and worldwide

Astara
792 W. Arrow Highway
Upland, CA 91786
(909) 981-4941; fax (909) 920-9541
info@astara.org
www.astara.org
Dedicated to elevating the consciousness and health of humankind.

Self-Realization Fellowship
Founded by Paramahansa Yogananda, 1920
The Mother Center
3880 San Rafael Avenue, Dept. 9W
Los Angeles, CA 90065-3298
(323) 225-2471
www.yogananda-srf.org
Additional centers in the United States and worldwide.

Suggested Reading

Bro, Harmon Hartzell. *Edgar Cayce on Dreams.* Edited by Hugh L. Cayce.
New York: Warner Books, 1995.
Carlson, H. G. *Mysteries of the Unexplained.* Chicago: Contemporary
Books, 1994.
Cerminara, Gina. *Many Mansions: The Edgar Cayce Story on
Reincarnation.* New York: New American Library, 1999.

Harner, Michael J. *The Way of the Shaman*. San Francisco: Harper San Francisco, 1990.

Montgomery, Ruth. *A Search for the Truth*. New York: Fawcett Books, 1992.

Stearn, Jess. *Edgar Cayce: The Sleeping Prophet*. New York: Bantam Books, 1990.

———. *Yoga, Youth, and Reincarnation*. New York: A.R.E. Press, 1997.

Sugrue, Thomas. *The Story of Edgar Cayce: There Is a River*. Rev. ed. New York: A.R.E. Press, 1997.

Yogananda, Paramahansa. *Autobiography of a Yogi*. Los Angeles: Self-Realization Fellowship, 1979. (A life-transforming book.)

Zolar. *Zolar's Encyclopedia and Dictionary of Dreams*. New York: Simon & Schuster, 1992.

Books, Tapes, and Resources by Joyce Keller

All resources are available at www.joycekeller.com.

Keller, Joyce. *Calling All Angels!: 57 Ways to Invite Angels into Your Life*. Avon, Mass.: Adams Media Corporation, 2000.

Keller, Joyce, and Jack Keller. *The Complete Book of Numerology*. New York: St. Martin's Press, 2001.

Keller, Joyce, and Elaine Keller Beardsley. *Karmascopes: Steps to Overcoming Life's Challenges*. More information at www.elainebeardsley.com.

Joyce Keller Online
Joyce Keller's monthly Love/Relationship Forecast:
   www.lifetimetv.com
   aol keyword: "Joyce Keller"
   www.lifetimetv.com/astro/
Joyce Keller's Ask the Astrologer:
   http://www.lifetimetv.com/astro/advice/_ask.html
Joyce Keller's Lifetime Chats:
   http://www.lifetimetv.com/community/chat/joycekeller_artist.html
Joyce Keller's Daily Horoscope:
   http://www.lifetimetv.com/astro/advice/index.html

Other Guides and Tapes
Joyce's Love & Sex Compatibility Wheel
   Great fun, accurate, too, for understanding old or new relationships.
How to Channel
   Guided meditation tape using Seven Steps to Heaven Connection Technique. Use it to connect with loved ones, teachers, guides, and your angels.
Heart Hunting: Be a Love Magnet!
   Connect with the soul mate of your dreams (tape). Joyce's secret, easy, time-tested techniques.

Healing Tape
Directions on healing from within and without. Miracles have been reported.

How to Contact Your Angels and Departed Loved Ones (Tape)
Safe and wonderful.

Psychic Secrets I (Tape)
Increase your ESP. Deep relaxation. Purpose of life, what happens before birth, channeling, truth about reincarnation, and guided meditation.

Psychic Secrets II (Tape)
Breath and body control. End stress and fatigue. Meditation and past-life regression. Truth about death.

Weight Loss Tape
Unusual, inspired, and incredibly effective.

Prosperity Tape
Universal abundance can be yours. Joyce leads you through proven steps that are guaranteed to work for you. Your angels are at your side!

Additional Resources

These sites are included to help you on your search. Inclusion does not constitute an endorsement.

Dream Recall
"The Mind Brain Lab: International Experiments in Consciousness": www.omnimag.com/archives/mind_brain/dream/
Electronic Voice Phenomena/Instrumental Transcommunication
    American Association of Electronic Voice Phenomena
    http://dreamwater.com/aaevp/index.html
World ITC
    www.worldit.org

Labyrinths
"How to Draw/Build a Classic Minoan Labyrinth," by Mary DeDanan.
    www.westbynorthwest.org/summer00/labyrnth/how/index.shtml
The Labyrinth Society (to find a labyrinth near you):
    www.labyrinthsociety.org; (877) 446-4520
Lessons for Living (fingertip labyrinth patterns):
    www.lessons4living.com/labyrinth.htm
Mid-Atlantic Geomancy: www.geomancy.org
Prairiewoods Franciscan Spirituality Center:
    www.prairiewoods.org
Relax4life (finger labyrinths, labyrinth kits):
    www.labyrinthproducts.com/index.htm

Crystal Tones
(800) 358-9492 or (801) 486-6833
www.crystalbowls.com

Lily Dale Assembly
5 Melrose Park
Lily Dale, NY 14752
(716) 595-8721
www.lilydale.org

Prayer Bead Kits
Land of Odds
522 East Iris Drive
Nashville, TN 37204
(615) 292-0610
www.landofodds.com

Sacred Gems
11432 South Street, #127
Cerritos, CA 90703
(562) 402-3537
gurukirn@sacredgems.com
www.sacredgems.com

Sacred Dance
Tribe, by Gabrielle Roth
The Moving Center
P.O. Box 271, Cooper Station
New York, NY 10276
(212) 760-1381, fax (212) 760-1387
ravenrec@panix.com; www.raven-
recording.com/ravenrec

Shamanic Studies
Foundation for Shamanic Studies
P.O. Box 1939
Mill Valley, CA 94942
(415) 380-8282
info@shamanicstudies.com
www.shamanicstudies.com

Singing Bowls (Crystal)
Singing Rainbow
P.O. Box 10297
Houston, TX 77206
(713) 681-9655
http://discoverthesound.com
   /sys-tmpl/door

Singing Bowls (Tibetan)
Tenzin's Imports
33 Arthur Avenue, SE
Minneapolis, MN 55414
(612) 378-9538
www.oldyak.com

Spirit Camps
Camp Chesterfield
P.O. Box 132
Chesterfield, IN 46017
(765) 378-0235
www.campchesterfield.net

Silk Circles (also spirit cabinet and
other metaphysical work)
United Metaphysical Churches
1488 Peters Creek Road, NW
Roanoke, VA 24017
(540) 562-4889
www.amcchapel.org
(above website for
Arlington Metaphysical Church
contains a reference to United
Metaphysical Churches)

Printed in the United States
By Bookmasters